LEO

JULY 21–AUGUST 21

2003

JOVE BOOKS, NEW YORK

The publishers regret that they cannot answer individual letters requesting personal horoscope information.

2003 TOTAL HOROSCOPE: LEO

PRINTING HISTORY
Jove edition / June 2002

Visit our website at
www.penguinputnam.com

ISBN: 0-515-13317-5

A JOVE BOOK®
Jove Books are published by The Berkley Publishing Group,
a division of Penguin Putnam Inc.,
375 Hudson Street, New York, New York 10014.
JOVE and the "J" design
are trademarks belonging to Penguin Putnam Inc.

PRINTED IN THE UNITED STATES OF AMERICA

10 9 8 7 6 5 4 3 2 1

CONTENTS

MESSAGE TO LEO

Dear Leo,

Never forget how important love is, for Leo is the sign of love. It warms you, nourishes you, fills you with strength, renews your will to live. Love is life for you. You need it and feel you deserve it. Your heart demands it and your whole being emits a very real radiance when you feel love and are loving someone.

Ideally you are a passionate person, a romantic gambler with a flair for seeking and finding a love partner. It is one for your major interests, probably the most important issue in your development. Of course, everybody wants love; everybody needs it.

No matter what your birthdate is, if you're a Leo you're a lover. Male or female. Young or old. Your sex or age doesn't alter the powerful passion and drama surrounding your life. You're always ready to try a new experience and you love to flirt and play the field. If you're the boasting type, chances are your self-confidence is suffering. Sexually, when there are disappointments and confusions you tend to take them as blows to your self-image, which you like to keep as positive and optimistic as possible.

You are dashing and bold and cut a sexy figure. Proud and noble, your bearing reflects the trace of regal blood that exists somewhere in your veins. You'll gamble if you see someone you're attracted to. It excites you to be attractive to someone else and, when it's mutual, you become a knight in shining armor, a pioneer, an adventurer—a hero crossing great distances, braving real dangers, cutting through jungle after jungle, doing anything you can to be near your heart's desire. The elements of drama, danger, and high intensity prolong the life of your affairs. You delight in bringing a quality to others' lives that they cannot find anywhere else. In that sense, you must be their central source of emotional sustenance. You usually don't tolerate being second or third, and if life puts you in a position of being other than the favorite, the radiant beauty of your warm and loving personality becomes a scorching violence that can cause irreparable damage to those you love and to yourself.

You have a high sense of honor and will deny your loved one nothing. You find your joy in lighting up the lives of your chosen loved ones. You're a great provider and extend yourself to the limit to make sure that enjoyment is present in your affairs and that no whim or idea need be curtailed for lack of adequate funds or means. Pleasure, relaxation, and fun are basic elements of your personality, and anyone connected with you can look for these qualities. You are generous with everything you have, and are happy when you are sharing your blessings with the objects of your affection. You will buy the best gifts money can buy. You will offer vacations and trips. You will hand the Sun and Moon to anyone you love, because anything you do you want to do in the biggest, most spectacular way. You could make rash promises, sincere at the time because they are born out of love, but time and circumstances could make it difficult for you to deliver when the moment of truth comes.

Your romance and idealism are irresistible, and the brilliance and intensity of your ardent pursuit of someone is hard to turn down. You can put stars in anyone's eyes if you put your mind to it. Not only do you take a sportsman's joy in the chase, but you have the competitive nature of wanting to be a winner. Winning the game becomes your single-minded objective, and so the heart of your passion rises. As you get more determined to win, you turn on more, get more excited. Everything is magnified, including your promises. You get carried away with the feelings, the hopes, the optimism of all that is possible. You make sure the person you love won't forget you. You want love and you know how to get it.

When you don't get absolute devotion, there's trouble. If your love life's bad, there's a problem with your self-image that needs correcting. Either you lack confidence and feel guilty and undeserving of affection, or your past deeds (or devotion to your own ego) now turn around to remind you of what you must become. You are demanding and domineering, and your bossy intolerant nature is hard for many people to bear. You are stubborn and unyielding. Although you possess a profoundly loving nature, you often interpret independence in others as mutiny against yourself. When you smell mutiny, you crack down like a panicky commanding officer. You tighten your grip with a maniacal need to control and continue to be the central force. How dare anyone just go off and do what they please? What about you?

It isn't that you don't understand the need for independence. Quite the contrary. You cannot really take orders from anyone but yourself. When you find yourself in situations that require your unquestioning obedience, you are miserable. When you meet conditions that demand your loyalty, you rebel. You prefer your loyalty to be a loudly proclaimed emotion you alone have generated. You will not tolerate its legislation. Yet you expect to be the prime source of love and life for others. If they take one step in either direction without your permission, you react. Many times you compensate for this strong authoritarian streak in your personality by creating live-and-let-live situations in which you don't question other people's actions and they don't question yours. It's a kind of hands-off democracy you set up. It gives you the freedom you want to explore life as you see fit, but actually democracy is not your true philosophy. If anything, you prefer to be an enlightened despot. Grandiose, inspiring, and proud, you must ultimately grant freedom to others, for your primary desire is to have freedom yourself. Although you are a seeker of truth, your baser side may care little for justice or personal freedom, as long as you are getting all the attention you think you deserve. You squawk like an infant and spare no tirades, tantrums, or histrionics to regain attention or control. When you calm down quickly and turn the smile back on you're given what you want.

Yours is an ego trip, all right. At worst you lack integrity and will do anything, absolutely anything, for attention and to come out looking good, no matter where the blame gets placed for whatever goes wrong. In that sense you are the cowardly Lion. You fear what others will think and cannot stand to have anyone believe that you are not noble, forthright, honorable, courageous, efficient, and capable. You will resort to deviousness, ironically enough, to make sure it doesn't look like you've been devious. You can be boastful, a thoughtless show-off obsessed with covering your egocentric insecurities with a false display of bravado. Your feelings may lack depth and you can lose your emotional integrity because you get too involved with your image.

At best you are conscious of your position and never abuse it. You recognize your worth and capitalize on it. Your potentials are unlimited and you know it. You have the capacity to be a great lover and you are aware of it. You like to be depended on. You enjoy having the spotlight. You like to be admired for your talents. You love being able to offer somebody a good time. You develop yourself best as a warm, inspiring individual, positive and aggressive and filled with love, honor, and charity. The flame of adventure burns deep within your soul and you provide a strong courageous light to guide others. When courage, stamina, and constancy are called for, there you will be. When supportive life-giving energy is needed, you are on hand to provide it. Your strong nature and supreme will are the foundations of life for all those around you.

You love your children but may see them as reflections of yourself. You expect a lot from them and have a difficult time accepting their individuality with all their complexities and needs, their different aspects of personality. You are devastated when they make the same mistakes you made, or make what you think are unnecessary blunders. But you are all too aware of what it means to be stubborn and headstrong. You also know how vital it is for each person to get his chance to show his potential and develop the talents he thinks he has, with no interference from anybody. You don't want to cause anxiety or uncertainty in your children or to hamper their development with guilt. Yet you expect so much. Yes, you're proud to say you expect a lot. But the relationship between parent and child is one of your secret sources of sorrow.

You often have feelings of great confusion when it comes to home, family, and children. Although you are a loving, devoted parent who tries to present a good strong image for children to follow, you would often prefer them to do as you say, not as you do. As much as you love your home and family, you have to escape it at the same time. You want your home and family to be the best examples of happiness and success that your friends can peek in the window and see. You pride yourself in your children and your relationships and want your marriage to be filled with love, respect, and joy. Your home reflects the glow of your success and you are proud of it.

But you still escape from them all. Why? What is this nagging fear you have of being dependent on a family? Time and time again you'll go off, running away either geographically or mentally, only to be drawn back again by irreconcilable conflicts, guilt, worries, and inexorable responsibilities. Your self-image depends largely on your projection of yourself as the courageous, independent Lion, out on his or her own for the first time. There is a newness to your approach, a youthful vigor and fresh-hatched quality that implies you have left home behind. You detest being thought of as dependent or attached to anybody's apron strings. And so you'll assert yourself time and again to affirm your statement of individuality and selfhood. Your own childhood and your attitude toward it, your own relationship to your parents, are often tinged with bittersweet sorrow.

You're a sucker for flattery, so watch out. But the truth is, your talents are almost unlimited. If you're not doing something with all your potential, you'll find someone to blame, to be sure. Since failure is a concept you cannot accept, you must find a suitable place to look for responsibility. Either your parents were too strict or they weren't strict enough, or some obligation or responsibility did this or that to you, or whatever. Actually, you are more the master of your own destiny than most people around you. At some point you will stand up, shake the cobwebs off your image, and get out there and show the world how it's done—bravely and responsibly.

Leo is the sign of show business and entertainment. You love to make people laugh and be happy, hypnotizing them with the magic of theater. You have as much if not more creative talent than any artist of your day, yet you are sometimes more taken with the image of being an artist than with the commitment and discipline of being one. But your sign is ruler of all forms of amusement, pleasure, and entertainment. Creativity is one of your key words. There is something shining in you. Don't be bashful about it. (You're really not bashful anyway.) It's there, it's real, and it's something unique that needs to be expressed. You're on stage all the time anyway, forever acting a leading role. But in actual theater it's hard for you to erase yourself long enough to assume the personality presented by the character in the play. Whatever this special talent is, at some point in your life it will have to come out and be recognized—maybe not by half the population of the world, although that would be nice. You want to be recognized, loved, and appreciated for the true gifts you feel you have to offer.

In your career, people naturally like you. You are charming, seductive, and persuasive when you're feeling confident. In your ruthless moments you will set the stage for disaster just so everyone can count on you. But you are a truth-seeker at heart, with a winning manner that reflects your honesty and sincerity. You're a born leader with a commanding, decisive approach that makes people listen. When you have facts and knowledge and experience to back up your enthusiasm, you can't lose.

You're a thoughtful but demanding boss, at your best when you are diplomatically frank and gently exacting. Barking orders and screaming directions may postpone but ultimately cause the mutiny you so abhor. Your extreme self-involvement will make it necessary to have helpers around. The more thoughtful you are of them, the more they'll want to do for you. Your position can be enhanced by your bold willingness to take chances and your ability to command respect. People automatically look up to you, and your firm, resolute acceptance of authority and responsibility will lead you away from the employ of others and toward your own enterprises.

Although you are a born comedian and love the spotlight, you often work behind the scenes and control even the stars who are out there performing. You can manage, manipulate, and cajole. Your talent for creating images brings you success in fields of art, entertainment, and business. You have an unmatchable talent to produce, and this must be exercised. For years you may operate by helping others, doing things for others' careers, advancing their stations, and giving of yourself for others. Your generous spirit opens your heart to those who need you, and you rarely say no.

Yet eventually you must express your own talent, develop what you have to offer, make your creative emotional statement to the world.

You'll be called a bigmouthed show-off. You'll be told to pipe down. You'll be labeled a glory hound and big shot. You may have trouble in school or getting a formal education. But talent is there, not just talent to dominate and feed your all-consuming inferiority-superiority complex, but real potential to light the way for others and give joy and pleasure to the world. That quality is personal integrity.

In all your relationships with people, this will be the factor that nourishes a partnership or poisons it. You need a partner who will adore you but who will be able to deal with your childish insecurities. You need a person to stand by you and assess you honestly, not just blindly flatter your foppish vanity. You need someone who can stand apart from you when you get too bossy, someone who can understand you when nobody else does. You need a person who believes in freedom and needs a little separation once in a while. But what will inspire love the most is someone who recognizes your sense of integrity and helps you build it, giving you the old victory sign when you need it. You are you, for better or worse. You love it, actually, and you need to be proud of loving yourself. The healthier you are about enjoying that feeling of strong selfhood, the less likely you will be to beat people over the head with yourself.

It isn't just a sick narcissistic love affair between you and you. It's got to be more than vulgar egotism. It has to be a recognition of some cosmic force of light and life that you personify.

The integrity you feel as an individual is your great achievement. Express the truth of your feelings.

Michael Lutin

LEO SNEAK PREVIEW OF THE
21st CENTURY

As the decade opens on a new century, indeed on a new millennium, the planets set the stage for change and challenge. Themes connecting present and future are in play. Already, planetary influences that emerged from the century just past are showing the drama unfolding in the twenty-first century. These influences reveal hidden paths and personal hints for achieving your potential—your message from the planets.

Leo individuals, ruled by the Sun, are coming out of a period of obstacles, restrictions, and delays. Ahead are hope and idealism to put the past behind and to set out on a positive course. Pluto in Sagittarius late 1995 into the year 2008 is your guide. Sagittarius, a fire sign compatible with your fiery nature, symbolizes the search for truth, a love of wisdom, and, eventually, self-understanding. Pluto in Sagittarius starts uncovering the truth by impacting your emotions, sentiment, memory. It brings up issues of caring and nurturing, learning and teaching. Home life, family, and children are brought sharply into focus.

Another feature of the Sagittarius influence is education. You may be studying or inventing theory. You may be pursuing rigorous training in academia, the art scene, or the athletic arena. New ideas and techniques come easily. But what you learn cannot be limited to a small personal world or to an insulated family. Press to reach the larger community. Fire sign Sagittarius also augments the urge to travel. Have a specific goal at journey's end, or much energy and money can be wasted. Most of all, beware of wasting your unique vision in scattered starts and halts.

Saturn, planet of discipline, channels your vision. Saturn focuses energy and brings you down to earth. Saturn inexorably modifies expansive Sagittarius and its ruler Jupiter even while Jupiter transits the signs. Jupiter in Gemini to midsummer 2001 stimulates Leo expressive talents. Jupiter in Cancer to midsummer 2002 provides a rich medium for creativity. Jupiter in your sign of Leo through late August 2003 swells the possibilities for success.

Saturn's own transit through the signs acts as a sobering influence. Saturn in Taurus till spring 2001 blends practicality and imagination. Saturn in Gemini to summer 2003 creates a structure for spontaneity. Saturn, a co-ruler of Aquarius, always has significance for Leo because Leo is cosmically linked to Aquarius.

The air sign of Aquarius is your zodiacal mate as well as zodiacal opposite. Here are important lessons for the twenty-first century. Aquarius poses involvement in the larger community beyond ego, self, family, friends, associates. Saturn forms helpful aspects with genius planet Uranus, the other co-ruler of Aquarius, and also with visionary planet Neptune. Planets Uranus and Neptune have the potential to put Leo on a path of enlightenment in the new millennium.

Uranus in Aquarius early 1996 to 2003 mutes your individualistic bent, making you more group-minded. Neptune in Aquarius late 1998 to 2012 replaces fickle impulses and irresponsible relationships with loyal and trustworthy ties. With a strong belief in social reforms and with family and friends behind you, you can be a leader in the community. The humanitarianism of Aquarius lets you reach out and be at the center of the action to make the world a better place.

THE CUSP-BORN LEO

Are you *really* a Leo? If your birthday falls during the fourth week of July, at the beginning of Leo, will you still retain the traits of Cancer, the sign of the Zodiac before Leo? What if you were born late in August—are you more Virgo than Leo? Many people born at the edge, or cusp, of a sign have difficulty determining exactly what sign they are. If you are one of these people, here's how you can figure it out, once and for all.

Consult the table on page 17. Find the year you were born, and then note the day. The table will tell you the precise days on which the Sun entered and left your sign for the year of your birth. If you were born at the beginning or end of Leo, yours is a lifetime reflecting a process of subtle transformation. Your life on Earth will symbolize a significant change in consciousness, for you are either about to enter a whole new way of living or you are leaving one behind.

If you are a Leo, born during the fourth week of July, you may want to read the horoscope book for Cancer as well as Leo. Cancer holds the keys to many of your secret uncertainties and deep-rooted problems, and your secret needs and wishes. You are the spirit of independence and creativity, or want to be. Yet through Cancer you reveal your deep, but often hidden, need to have strong ties. You may be trying to leave dependencies behind, yet you find yourself drawn again and again to the past or to family responsibilities.

You reflect the birth of a new sign, a ripe, whole person, fully able to tap and realize all your potentials for love and creativity.

If you were born after the third week of August, you may want to read the horoscope book for Virgo as well, for through Virgo you learn to put all your talents as a lover or creator to work. Your love for life is infectious, and your zest and sunny disposition are an inspiration to everyone around you. You are capable of seriousness, discipline, and great diligence.

You are a lover—ardent, passionate, and determined that love will not elude you. Though you may try to avoid it, you will find yourself in work, health, or duty situations that demand less emotion and more mind. You are not afraid of taking a gamble and are reluctant to give up your love of enjoyment for work or studies. You can blend professionalism and propriety in perfect amounts. You are the natural mixture of creativity and discipline, able to feel and to analyze.

You symbolize the warmth and fullness of a late summer day, a natural ripeness and maturity that is mellow and comfortable to be near.

THE CUSPS OF LEO

DATES SUN ENTERS LEO
(LEAVES CANCER)

July 23 every year from 1900 to 2010,
except for the following:

July 22

1928	1960	1980	1994	2008
32	61	81	96	2009
36	64	84	97	2010
40	65	85	98	
44	68	86	2000	
48	69	88	2001	
52	72	89	2002	
53	73	90	2004	
56	76	92	2005	
59	77	93	2006	

DATES SUN LEAVES LEO
(ENTERS VIRGO)

August 23 every year from 1900 to 2010,
except for the following:

August 22				August 24	
1960	1980	1992	2001	1903	1919
64	84	93	2004	07	23
68	88	96	2005	11	27
72	89	97	2008	15	
76		2000	2009		

LEO RISING:
YOUR ASCENDANT

Could you be a "double" Leo? That is, could you have Leo as your Rising sign as well as your Sun sign? The tables on pages 20–21 will tell you Leos what your Rising sign happens to be. Just find the hour of your birth, then find the day of your birth, and you will see which sign of the Zodiac is your Ascendant, as the Rising sign is called. For a detailed discussion on how the Rising sign is determined, see pages 82–85.

Your Ascendant, or Rising sign, modifies your basic Sun sign personality, and it affects the way you act out the daily predictions for your Sun sign. If your Rising sign indeed is Leo, what follows is a description of its effect on your horoscope. If your Rising sign is some other sign of the Zodiac, you may wish to read the horoscope book for that sign as well.

With Leo Rising the planet on the Ascendant is the Sun. Here it may give you a special robustness—in appearance, in health, in spirit, in action—that you can count on long after your normal energy reserves are spent. On the negative side the Sun here may give you an overdose of pride and insolence, making you quick to resent or retaliate when reason instead should be the response.

A flair for the dramatic will be evident in the fabric of your life. You like managing people and events as long as you can play center stage, or at least create a powerful character part. You may weave intrigue if it provides an opportunity for you to take a leading role. Although you like pulling strings, your frank and generous disposition rises above petty disputes. You abhor superficial alliances and cliques.

Drama stamps your personal appearance, your possessions, your surroundings. You may adorn yourself and your environment as much for the effect it will create as for the comfort it will provide. Your appearance itself, whether natural or affected, runs to the high, the proud, and the bold. You can use physical gestures as signals—to lure, to persuade, to threaten. And because love, especially to be loved, is a fundament of your ego, your body language acts instinctively to attract people to you.

Your search for identity is usually not solitary or introspective. Public appreciation and power are essential to you. You need constant interaction and approval. You may find the most satisfying ties with groups whose goals are humanitarian and ideological. But first you may discvoer in youth and early adulthood many facets of yourself through creative activity. It is imperative for you with Leo Rising to create—a work of art, a child, an intrigue, a love affair, a partnership, or a principle.

Your need for people may reflect an inner insecurity. Your self-image may not be actualized until you see it mirrored in people's responses; a positive one reinforces enthusiasm, a negative one induces self-pity. Your need for creation may also be tied to the building of an ego. You seek success and are very likely to get your lion's share of it through what you do in your lifetime.

Above all, love and loyalty are the key words for you with Leo Rising to root yourself in your environment. Love and loyalty motivate your simplest act, your grandest attempt. They, too, can be the cause of pain and loss. You are happiest when you love and are loved in return.

RISING SIGNS FOR LEO

Hour of Birth*	Day of Birth		
	July 22–27	July 28–August 1	August 2–6
Midnight	Taurus	Taurus	Gemini
1 AM	Gemini	Gemini	Gemini
2 AM	Gemini	Gemini	Cancer
3 AM	Cancer	Cancer	Cancer
4 AM	Cancer	Cancer	Cancer
5 AM	Leo	Leo	Leo
6 AM	Leo	Leo	Leo
7 AM	Leo	Leo; Virgo 8/1	Virgo
8 AM	Virgo	Virgo	Virgo
9 AM	Virgo	Virgo	Virgo
10 AM	Libra	Libra	Libra
11 AM	Libra	Libra	Libra
Noon	Libra	Libra; Scorpio 7/30	Scorpio
1 PM	Scorpio	Scorpio	Scorpio
2 PM	Scorpio	Scorpio	Scorpio
3 PM	Sagittarius	Sagittarius	Sagittarius
4 PM	Sagittarius	Sagittarius	Sagittarius
5 PM	Sagittarius	Capricorn	Capricorn
6 PM	Capricorn	Capricorn	Capricorn
7 PM	Capricorn; Aquarius 7/26	Aquarius	Aquarius
8 PM	Aquarius	Aquarius	Aquarius; Pisces 8/3
9 PM	Pisces	Pisces	Pisces
10 PM	Aries	Aries	Aries
11 PM	Aries; Taurus 7/26	Taurus	Taurus

*Hour of birth given here is for Standard Time in any time zone. If your hour of birth was recorded in Daylight Saving Time, subtract one hour from it and consult that hour in the table above. For example, if you were born at 9 AM D.S.T., see 8 AM above.

Hour of Birth*	Day of Birth		
	August 7–11	**August 12–17**	**August 18–24**
Midnight	Gemini	Gemini	Gemini
1 AM	Gemini	Gemini	Cancer
2 AM	Cancer	Cancer	Cancer
3 AM	Cancer	Cancer	Cancer; Leo 8/22
4 AM	Leo	Leo	Leo
5 AM	Leo	Leo	Leo
6 AM	Leo	Leo; Virgo 8/16	Virgo
7 AM	Virgo	Virgo	Virgo
8 AM	Virgo	Virgo	Virgo; Libra 8/22
9 AM	Libra	Libra	Libra
10 AM	Libra	Libra	Libra
11 AM	Libra	Libra; Scorpio 8/14	Scorpio
Noon	Scorpio	Scorpio	Scorpio
1 PM	Scorpio	Scorpio	Scorpio; Sagittarius 8/22
2 PM	Sagittarius	Sagittarius	Sagittarius
3 PM	Sagittarius	Sagittarius	Sagittarius
4 PM	Sagittarius	Capricorn	Capricorn
5 PM	Capricorn	Capricorn	Capricorn
6 PM	Capricorn	Aquarius	Aquarius
7 PM	Aquarius	Aquarius	Pisces
8 PM	Pisces	Pisces	Pisces; Aries 8/21
9 PM	Aries	Aries	Aries
10 PM	Aries; Taurus 8/11	Taurus	Taurus
11 PM	Taurus	Taurus	Gemini

*See note on facing page.

LOVE AND RELATIONSHIPS

No matter who you are, what you do in life, or where your planets are positioned, you still need to be loved, and to feel love for other human beings. Human relationships are founded on many things: infatuation, passion, sex, guilt, friendship, and a variety of other complex motivations, frequently called love.

Relationships often start out full of hope and joy, the participants sure of themselves and sure of each other's love, and then end up more like a pair of gladiators than lovers. When we are disillusioned, bitter, and wounded, we tend to blame the other person for difficulties that were actually present long before we ever met. Without seeing clearly into our own natures we will be quite likely to repeat our mistakes the next time love comes our way.

Enter Astrology.

It is not always easy to accept, but knowledge of ourselves can improve our chances for personal happiness. It is not just by predicting when some loving person will walk into our lives, but by helping us come to grips with our failures and reinforce our successes.

Astrology won't solve all our problems. The escapist will ultimately have to come to terms with the real world around him. The hard-bitten materialist will eventually acknowledge the eternal rhythms of the infinite beyond which he can see or hear. Astrology does not merely explain away emotion. It helps us unify the head with the heart so that we can become whole individuals. It helps us define what it is we are searching for, so we can recognize it when we find it.

Major planetary cycles have been changing people's ideas about love and commitment, marriage, partnerships, and relationships. These cycles have affected virtually everyone in areas of personal involvement. Planetary forces point out upheavals and transformations occurring in all of society. The concept of marriage is being totally reexamined. Exactly what the changes will ultimately bring no one can tell. It is usually difficult to determine which direction society will take. One thing is certain: no man is an island. If the rituals and pomp of wedding ceremonies must be revised, then it will happen.

Social rules are being revised. Old outworn institutions are indeed crumbling. But relationships will not die. People are putting less stress on permanence and false feelings of security. The emphasis now shifts toward the union of two loving souls. Honesty, equality, and mutual cooperation are the goals in modern marriage. When these begin to break down, the marriage is in jeopardy. Surely there must be a balance between selfish separatism and prematurely giving up.

There is no doubt that astrology can establish the degree of compatibility between two human beings. Two people can share a common horizon in life but have quite different habits or basic interests. Two others might have many basic characteristics in common while needing to approach their goals from vastly dissimilar points of view. Astrology describes compatibility based on these assumptions.

It compares and contrasts through the fundamental characteristics that draw two people together. Although they could be at odds on many basic levels, two people could find themselves drawn together again and again. Sometimes it seems that we keep being attracted to the same type of individuals. We might ask ourselves if we have learned anything from our past mistakes. The answer is that there are qualities in people that we require and thus seek out time and time again. To solve that mystery in ourselves is to solve much of the dilemma of love, and so to help ourselves determine if we are approaching a wholesome situation or a potentially destructive one.

We are living in a very curious age with respect to marriage and relationships. We can easily observe the shifting social attitudes concerning the whole institution of marriage. People are seeking everywhere for answers to their own inner needs. In truth, all astrological combinations can achieve compatibility. But many relationships seem doomed before they get off the ground. Astrologically there can be too great a difference between the goals, aspirations, and personal outlook of the people involved. Analysis of both horoscopes must and will indicate enough major planetary factors to keep the two individuals together. Call it what you will: determination, patience, understanding, love—whatever it may be, two people have the capacity to achieve a state of fulfillment together. We all have different needs and desires. When it comes to choosing a mate, you really have to know yourself. If you know the truth about what you are really looking for, it will make it easier to find. Astrology is a useful, almost essential, tool to that end.

In the next chapter your basic compatibility with each of the twelve signs of the Zodiac is generalized. The planetary vibrations between you and an individual born under any given zodiacal sign suggest much about how you will relate to each other. Hints are provided about love and romance, sex and marriage so that you and your mate can get the most out of the relationship that occupies so important a role in your life.

LEO:
YOU AND YOUR MATE

LEO—ARIES

A strong bond exists between you two. Once you have survived the wars waged by your egos, it will be hard to pry you apart emotionally. You are both idealistic, emotional creatures governed by the power of creation and the love of life. Love is your great source of energy, and you cannot thrive without it. Your capacity to love each other as well as yourselves is limitless. Self-involved and demanding, you can have storms and raging battles yet somehow remain loyal through it all. You are adventurous, passionate, and ardent. You make a very glamorous couple.

Ambitious and dynamic, you are both imbued with the fighting spirit and the joy of living that make whatever you do radiant with the strength of your combined spirit. As a team, whatever you dedicate yourselves to will no doubt be a success, provided selfishness and ego don't expand faster than your mutual understanding. Leo may play the baby for a long long time, but Aries will continue to love—tantrums, flirtations, and bossiness notwithstanding. You are usually grateful to have that strong Aries influence to help make dreams come true, and take new chances in life.

Hints for Your Aries Mate

This is a royal match, and you Leos better make sure you treat your Aries mate with every appearance, let alone act, of equally shared power. Aries will often play the prince, the minister, to your sovereign moods. But never underestimate the authority that your Aries partner holds and will wield if the relationship gets unruly. Allow Aries his or her sternness in your behalf; it will keep your partnership going in tandem longer than dramatic emotion or playful sexuality will. Speaking of the latter, you can always entice your lover on those levels, and it's good for Aries to feel the fun side of sex and the serious side of emotion. Often brusque and humorless when threatened, Aries will respond to your kittenish ways home alone after a hard day's work. If you've had an awful day, too, tell Aries so, and let your mate once again minister to your feelings, your problems, and your solutions. Take turns being the leader.

LEO—TAURUS

Truly a long-lasting possibility. More than just an endurance contest, you are the unified picture of loyalty, faithfulness, and honorable love.

You are both lusty, pleasure-oriented people. Taurus finds pleasure through earthly tastes for luxury and wealth and the best money can buy. Leo finds pleasure through the fiery joys of giving happiness to loved ones. You can provide a combined atmosphere of rigidity and warmth, wealth and coziness, moved by your need for status and security.

Worldly success and speculation will enter your relationship, for the passion and glamour that dazzle you both can be cooled by the harsh realities of financial liabilities and unexpected reversal. Though you are drawn together for sexual fulfillment, tender security, and worldly encouragement, you may find the opposite: frustration, insecurity, and discouragement. Yet you are both fortified with a sense of stamina, endurance, and strong codes of honor and loyalty. Great transformations can occur between you, eye-openers when you can see farther than you've ever seen before, understanding what you have never imagined, knowing something about the world and the universe beyond your sheltered lives.

Hints for Your Taurus Mate

As much as you honor the traditional, and as much as your Taurus mate agrees with you, you will have a more fulfilling relationship with Taurus if you explore the unfamiliar, follow an unorthodox route. Basically that means not paying too much attention to the physical things in your home life. Your union with Taurus should not be on account of material luxuries and comforts, though Taurus is always telling you how she or he likes to revel in those things. Food and sex do not have to be expensive or exotic to be imaginative. You do not need a velvet loveseat for the livingroom; a hammock or swing is where you and Taurus can share your most intimate thoughts. Find glamour in places where flirtation and peer pressure do not threaten. Book passage for two aboard a tramp steamer, if any exist, or join a collective farm where you and your Taurus mate can really get down to planting, weeding, hoeing, and harvesting.

LEO—GEMINI

You are cosmically linked and thus you have a natural attraction and the ability to have a harmonious relationship. Together you can reflect certainty, stability, enduring warmth and love, and gracious, cheerful acceptance of people. You are the marriage of creativity and intelligence and can express during the course of your relationship the blend of the conservative with the unusual.

At worst, your conflicts can bring out your flippant

game playing, perverse rebelliousness, and childish tantrums. It can be a serious war between honest commitment and superficial philandering, flagrant rule breaking and harsh, domineering authoritarianism. The more restless one becomes the more fearful of change you both grow. You can damage your partnership irreparably if you treat your partner's need for individual growth as mutiny. You can harm yourselves if you resist stability and regularity.

You need to unite regularity with change. You can excite each other sexually and emotionally and should always strive to elicit warmth and trust from each other. Yours is the growth from adolescence to maturity, from egotistical self-containment to mutual understanding and the experiencing of greater horizons.

Hints for Your Gemini Mate

This balmy union between you fire-ruled Leos and your airy Gemini mates needs constant sunshine and sultry breezes to make it work. Give up a little of your leonine aloofness, unbend to Gemini. The warmth of your confidences will arouse Gemini's curiosity which, once satisfied, turns to sympathy. Talk should be the mainstay of your relationship. You can keep that summertime romance going by always opening up to your Gemini partner. Neither pride nor pique nor privacy should hold you back from being totally free. Don't ever be afraid to show how upset you are. Gemini is splendid in an emergency. Expressing your ideas and feelings has an erotic effect on your Gemini partner, whose idea of perfect sexual communion is immediately after a gabfest. You'll have a lot of sex, and a lot of love, with this advice, for Gemini becomes haplessly ensnared with the person who shares the most of his or her inner self.

LEO—CANCER

You can provide light and warmth for the whole world. Ideally, your union combines the power and virility of the traditional heroic male with the sympathy and fertility of the traditional female. Together you have a sense of justice, candor, and honesty that keeps your relationship stable and secure. You can distribute responsibilities and cares between you, so that a constant source of love is generated between you, flowing outward to those around you. Sexually you can be a masterful combination. You are both imbued with powerful basic drives and the universal human need to feel emotional fulfillment through passionate and joyful union.

At worst, your relationship can be a sick play on insecurities, enslavement by an egotistical domineering despot, a subtle war between domestic guilt and personal control, between a strict parent and a child running away from home. To be fruitful, you must defend and support Cancer, and Cancer must quietly stand behind your decisions.

This is a highly spiritual blend of life forces, a productive possibility for happiness.

Hints for Your Cancer Mate

Like the gentle rain, the calm meandering streams of summertime, like a shaded, gradual clime, your Cancer mate is slowly warmed by your glow. A blaze of emotion, like the hot, hot sun, will simmer, seethe, and swirl your lover's emotions. After Cancer has let off the steam, she or he may retreat from you for a while. Come back again with gentle radiance. Put pride aside. Don't nurture your private hurts either, for that cold, cold sun will frost and ice the sentiments your Cancer mate is stewing about. Emotion is the area you Leos must handle with kid gloves around your Cancer partner. The rest of your relationship will fall into place easily. Focus on the things that keep you together—money, food, a sense of history. Even though you think differently about them, sharing them in your unique ways brings your past up to date, and sets the present in perspective for the future.

LEO—LEO

You both need special treatment and royal handling. Each of you needs attention and a lot of ego bolstering. Both need to feel loved, wanted, and desired for the warmth and strength of your supportive love. Role playing may interfere with togetherness in this union, for you both need to be the central power source. Ego clashes and too many similarities may make this a difficult match.

When this combination is successful, it is often because one of you is the mischief maker and one is the authority figure. When one of you remains central and stable, the other can depend on that stability, guidance and control. At worst, you can behave like two children, competing for attention, scrapping and scrambling to salvage your own precious egos.

At best, you are two loving souls, noble creatures meeting on the battlefield of love and matching desire for desire, passion for passion. You can give each other inspiration, dignity, and most of all freedom to develop your talents and express your true potentials.

If one of you was born between July 20 and August 1, prepare for a power-packed relationship. There will be new trips, new horizons, long-term changes in goals and relationships, with many wild, unexpected turns of fate. Both of you can benefit from this tremendous energy potential.

Hints for Your Leo Mate

You are attracted to each other like two moths to a flame—the same Leo flame. Yet you may be so courteous and fair with each other that neither of you ever gets close enough to the flame, or to each other, to be burned. That's good if your relationship is supposed to be on that joyous, platonic level. But if you, or one of you, want more, you'll have to search your nature deeply to do it. Humor, ease, letting be, and letting go characterize your union. Keep these, but add serious purpose. One of you has to let the other Leo know that without love and deep commitment to that love, your union is mostly stage setting that can be easily upset when a new star contends for the scene. You two veteran actors should share the hard knocks, the disappointments, the weariness and emptiness of glitter and popularity so that you can truly fulfill each other's real needs: work and love in tandem.

LEO—VIRGO

Together you are a remarkable mixture of hot and cold. You both need romance, warmth, and affection and both of you are capable of passion and fantasy. Together you have a seductive blend of crude emotion and refined sensibilities. You both need some distance from each other to regain control of your own lives. Honor and practicality color your emotional lives, and after feelings boil over and passions cool, you are better able to make decisions and put yourselves in order, putting aside manipulative rivalries.

Yours is the union of glamour and pragmatism, warm thrills and cool chills, good times and sober times, love and work. At worst, you can be the unhealthy combination of a despotic ruler and a resentful servant. At best, you symbolize the union of the creative lover and the dedicated artisan, turning your talents into tangible, useful gains.

This is primarily the marriage of love and work. When you conquer ego pride and fearful hypercriticism, you can reach a period of prosperous fulfillment in association. Together you represent maturity—the ripeness of a harvest time—and when united properly you can harvest a rich crop together and separately.

Hints for Your Virgo Mate

In general, you Leo lovers must distinguish between friskiness and peskiness with your Virgo mates. Virgo can be captivated by your loving vibes. That warm, sincere voice—use it a lot, Virgo likes to listen and learn. Those silky, pleading hands—don't paw, Virgo is fastidious. That robust, invigorating lust—don't eat too much, drink too much, or sleep too late, for Virgo is too alert, lean, and efficient to let you get away with sloppiness. Never whine with a Virgo. State your resentments in the most resolute manner. That will get your Virgo mate thinking rationally about the solutions, and will ensure that she or he is absolutely loyal to your cause. And you better show loyalty up front and in private with Virgo, otherwise you're done for. One of your natural Leo traits that always keeps Virgo happy is entertaining in public with friends, as long as you're your regal best.

LEO—LIBRA

You've got the possibility of a warm, loving, and responsive relationship. Together you can share affection, companionship, security, and financial success. Deep down, you are both friendly, harmonious people and can be considerate as well as passionate. It's a comfortable connection at best, sometimes as close as brother and sister.

You've got to contend with ego that can be revoltingly insatiable or controlling, and a superficial, calculated playfulness that can take real joy and fire out of living. You may get bored and restless. If you do, the relationship can degenerate into a meaningless interchange that skirts basic issues and problems. It can be a contest of arrogance and vanity, pomp and flattery, where you spend half your time puffing up an ego and the other half knocking it down.

At best, you are true companions, at times a little detached but friendly. You can be the perfect combination for love and marriage. You are the blend of stability and mutual support, the union of strength and weakness. When you change rude selfishness into stable, life-giving love, you will be most successful together. Strive to turn feelings of dependency into sincere consideration for your mate.

You and Your Libra Mate

You're the boss in this relationship with fair-minded Libra, who would rather have a boss than argue and call a confrontation. See that, know that, do that. Of course, if your bossiness ever gets vulgar or trite, Libra will leave you. But you Leos usually do not have to resort to street tactics. Your original jungle habitat makes you subtle, yet still able to cope with the inhabitants of the plains and the veldt. Subtlety is your best gambit with Libra. He or she likes to be lured into and out of things. But Libra is also a seasoned traveler of the open fields. Social, sociable, brilliant in company, liking a lot of gaiety and glamour, your Libra is easily won over if your whiskers are sleek, your tail high, and your mane smooth and flowing. In other words, be your brightest, most polished, gamest with your Libra partner in public. In private, you can roar. Be cuddly.

LEO—SCORPIO

You connect on deep emotional levels and can understand each other well, although you will not always agree. You are both aware of passion and desire. You both know how to survive crisis and how to emerge victorious from battle. You are connected by feeling, look up to one another, and find comfort and security in one another.

Sexually yours can be a steamy match, a hot-blooded surge of primitive drives and feelings. Though drawn to it, you cannot stand domination from each other, and your conflict will be as fierce as your passions are—when in the open. At worst, you battle for control and revenge. Jealousy, insecurity, and pain could take over this combination if you start to tap each other's strength—a ruthless power struggle that would be difficult to end once begun.

At best this is a tender loving match, filled with consideration and concern. You can help each other through crisis, nourish each other sexually and emotionally, and enrich each other's spirit. You're as primitive and powerful as love and death, and such a blend will imbue you both with the spirit of immortality. As tender as the bond between parent and child, this is a strong union, resistant to change and gifted with the power of regeneration.

Hints for Your Scorpio Mate

Keep doing with your Scorpio mate what you were fired to do when you first met him or her—warm those deep, cold, swirling undercurrents of emotion and ideology. You'll have to keep your hand in here, but unlike your Scorpio lover, don't hold your cards close to your chest. Leo is heart, and that's what Scorpio wants, even though she or he will do a thousand little things that on the surface seem rejecting or separative. Like the Sun, your own ruler, shining on the rivers and seas, shine on Scorpio. Make a fuss. Nurture with words, pats, caresses, snacks. Provide tidbits of gossip, propaganda, lofty ideas, grand plans. Then follow through when your Scorpio snaps at the bait. You must be free to follow Scorpio where your suggestions have led her or him. Don't shy away, kitteny and cute. Lions can stalk any terrain. Scorpio needs your fierce pride and unlimited courage to complete the journey.

LEO—SAGITTARIUS

You are always drawn to Sagittarius for that dreamer sparks your imagination and turns you on to your own talents. Together you can really accentuate the positive and eliminate the negative. Though you are both basically egocentric, you can develop a spirit of cooperation and mutual encouragement that can work miracles and assure you both of success. You both possess the love of life and the basic optimism that every relationship needs to grow to maturity. You are warm, generous creatures, capable of living together and yet separately, sharing tenderness and enthusiasm, helping each other develop skills with natural feeling and healthy buoyancy. You are an inspiration to each other.

At worst you can become wrapped up in your own worlds and egos, caught between selfishness and diffuse, unfocused excitement, bossy authoritarianism and permissive, unfilled meandering, indulgence and unrealistic dreams.

But at best together you can instead develop a blend of tact and candor, ingenuity and discipline, talent and wisdom. With its potentials for successfully manipulated risks, this is a high-stakes union where gambles must be taken. You join creativity, imagination, education, skill, and performance in areas of art, entertainment, publishing, learning, travel, speculation, and love itself.

Hints for Your Sagittarius Mate

Fire joins fire here. You Leos will kindle your Sagittarius mate's ideals, and vice versa. But when it comes down to bed and board, the fire may be nothing more than smoke and ashes. Who keeps the rent paid, who stocks the food supplies, who sees to it that family, friends, and neighbors get their due? These responsibilities must fall heavily on one of you flamboyant lovers. It might as well be you, Leo. Temper tantrums notwithstanding, your desire to succeed in the real world makes the dreams of your Sagittarius mate nursery rhymes in comparison. Don't neglect that nurturing aspect either, after you've done the day's work. Singing lullabys to your partner assures her or him of your love and also keeps the hopes and dreams alive. One day, when you've gotten beyond the here and now—which Sagittarius will require in a close partnership—you can go off and make those fantasies real.

LEO—CAPRICORN

At first you may think this is an unlikely combination, like moving a tropical island to the North Pole. But you two have many things in common and can bring each other to points of growth, development, and maturity. You both may fight a lot before you realize that. You'll complain about the constant demands—emotional or practical. You may encounter deadlocks or problems that will be insurmountable to younger or less mature members of your sign. You are both strong people. You like to be in control of your life. You don't like to feel that you're hardening, getting old or unattractive or over the hill. You both dislike feeling wildly out of control of your emotions and both of you are concerned with the image (or spectacle) you're making of yourself. You're ambitious, conservative people, imbued with the drive, determination, and stamina to get what you want.

When you don't get your own way, you can both turn ugly. Yet you are both honorable, constant, and desirous of doing your best and being great at whatever you do. Capricorn makes you work and points out all the unfinished tasks that you must get done in order for you to make it in the world. You turn Capricorn on, financially or sexually, and the pair can do a lot together. The relationship reflects your need to unify the hot and the cold within your own nature, to combine the passion of youth with the responsibility of a mature parent figure.

Hints for Your Capricorn Mate

You think you're shy in private, but you've seen nothing till you've seen your Capricorn mate freeze into reticence and isolation. That's where your Leo light and heat, which got you together in the first place, come right in. The big thaw is what's needed here. Usually reserved Capricorn will go for your sexual cavorting in a big way, directed solely to him or her, of course. Be sure you want the romp, for once aroused, your Capricorn lover will delight in having a tiger by the tail. Basically your relationship thrives in such intimate encounters as these. You won't have to worry much about the home, the social scene, the job. Share those burdens and joys with your Capricorn, because she or he is just as fit and just as traditional in those areas as you are. Raw love keeps you together; refinement graces it.

LEO—AQUARIUS

In the astrological scheme of things, Leo and Aquarius are zodiacal mates as well as zodiacal opposites. Both of you, being fixed signs, are stubborn. Leo looks to Aquarius for ideas, as Aquarius can view the realities of life with a broad philosophical view and maintain a progressive outlook. But Leo's high emotional pitch can frighten a detached Aquarius partner, who may resort to drastic measures.

You are perfect opposites. You join the qualities of a hot-blooded lover with the detachment of a scientist. Where one of you is well-ordered and dignified, needing stable planning and control, the other is disarrayed and ultracasual, craving spontaneity and unpredictability. Where one of you demands attention and obedience, the other turns wandering and rebellious.

But you complete each other perfectly and can symbolize the utter union and reconciliation of two opposing personalities. As long as you recognize each other's separateness, you can be joined. As long as you accept the fact that many of your partner's qualities are your qualities as well, you can welcome each other into your lives.

At worst, you can bring out cruelty and selfish domination or perverse, upsetting irresponsibility in each other. The more one becomes possessive and bossy, the further detached the partner becomes. The more one demands allegiance, the less support the other is able to give.

At best, you are the blend of a warm heart and intelligent mind. You can reflect the joys of a deep, private love and the human need for people, associations, and friendships outside the realms of usual love affairs.

Hints for your Aquarius Mate

You've found your Aquarius mate, because you've found someone as determined as you are, as up front as you are, as noble as you are, as addicted to social frills as serious purpose will allow. Think again when what you want together is a matter of private conflict! Aquarius will humor you for a while, but you won't think being kept in abeyance is so funny. So what happened to Leo? What happened to that open, game, playful lover that Aquarius always wanted? You got emotionally serious, but that's the last thing you can share with your Aquarius partner—emotions. It is you, Leo, who has to administer seriousness on a level that Aquarius can digest: pinches and dabs of strategy, spoonfuls of giving and taking, dashes of feeling. Please don't pour gusty expectations into the stew you're brewing with Aquarius. If you're patient, the partnership will cook to perfection.

LEO—PISCES

Though both your natures are warm, affectionate, and loving, you could remain strangers forever. Each of you may feel dominated and trapped, tied down and unable to take decisive actions because of your complex intertwined relationship. Actually, within each of you is a complex mixture of positive self-assurance and shy self-questioning. Together, you both blend the egomaniac with the selfless servant. You may feel under the thumb of a cruel demanding tyrant, or bound through guilt and responsibility to one who is weaker than you, helpless without you. Actually, this is the worst kind of Pisces-Leo relationship. You feed each other's feelings of total indispensability and worthless, confused incapacity. Yet you never let each other escape. You keep each other from growing strong or getting free.

At best, you are the perfect combination for creative expression. Together you blend the forces of mysticism, romance, and creativity. You can transform tortuous self-indulgence into spiritual strength. Emotionally and sexually, there's enough material there to marry and raise a family. Instead of resenting each other for what you are, try to maintain warmth. Together you have the capacity for love, generosity, passion, and tenderness—the whole spectrum of emotional feelings.

Hints for Your Pisces Mate

Even though you two agree on the big ideas, you won't agree with your Pisces mate's way of getting there. Loving mystery, which to you is just a series of clues and lures to pounce upon, your Pisces may deliver a staggeringly long list of maybes, nos, tomorrows, what ifs, on the other hands. Patience is a virtue you seldom exercise. Do so with your Pisces mate. All you are asked to sacrifice is your sense of timing. Pounce, okay, but do not prey; it's unfair for a cat to take advantage of a fish. Watch, listen, and learn. And when the big moment comes, take charge of the whole affair. You'll have a lot of practice at that, because in your union with Pisces you'll have to take charge of a lot of things from money-making, homemaking, to making dreams come true.

LEO:
YOUR PROGRESSED SUN

WHAT IS YOUR NEW SIGN

Your birth sign, or Sun sign, is the central core of your whole personality. It symbolizes everything you try to do and be. It is your main streak, your major source of power, vitality, and life. But as you live you learn, and as you learn you progress. The element in your horoscope that measures your progress is called the Progressed Sun. It is the symbol of your growth on Earth, and represents new threads that run through your life. The Progressed Sun measures big changes, turning points, and major decisions. It will often describe the path you are taking toward the fulfillment of your desires and goals.

Below you will find brief descriptions of the Progressed Sun in three signs. According to the table on page 43, find out about your Progressed Sun and see how and where you fit into the cosmic scheme. Each period lasts about 30 years, so watch and see how dramatic these changes turn out to be.

If Your Sun Is Progressing Into—

VIRGO, your sense of purpose gets more serious and you involve yourself with work in a wholehearted way. You must discipline yourself to produce, develop your talents, and perfect your crafts. You start using your head as well as your heart. You will turn toward healthier ways of living, and you will purify your life and live more simply. Your purpose becomes one of service.

LIBRA, you are graduating into the world, for now you enter into contacts with other people. You come to appreciate what others have to offer. You add diplomacy to your skills. You wish to marry, form partnerships, join your life with another. Cooperate with people and learn to assess, accept, and value them for what they really are.

SCORPIO, your passions and desires are awakened now as you cross the threshold into a world of intense and fertile creativity. Your powers of penetration will never be greater than they are during this segment of your life. Sex and sexuality become your key words and you come to understand death and life, mortality and immortality. Now you can slowly transform your entire nature so that you will be like the adult butterfly emerging from its cocoon.

HOW TO USE THE TABLE

Look for your birthday in the table on the facing page. Then under the appropriate column, find out approximately when your Progressed Sun will lead you to a new sign. From that point on, for 30 years, the thread of your life will run through that sign. Read the definitions on the preceding pages and see exactly how that life thread will develop.

For example, if your birthday is August 1, your Progressed Sun will enter Virgo around your 21st birthday and will travel through Virgo until you are 51 years old. Your Progressed Sun will then move into Libra. Reading the definitions of Virgo and Libra will tell you much about your major involvements and interests during those years.

YOUR PROGRESSED SUN

If your birthday falls on:	start looking at VIRGO at age	start looking at LIBRA at age	start looking at SCORPIO at age
July 21–23	30	60	90
24	29	59	89
25	28	58	88
26	27	57	87
27	26	56	86
28	25	55	85
29	24	54	84
30	23	53	83
31	22	52	82
August 1	21	51	81
2	20	50	80
3	19	49	79
4	18	48	78
5	17	47	77
6	16	46	76
7	15	45	75
8	14	44	74
9	13	43	73
10	12	42	72
11	11	41	71
12	10	40	70
13	9	39	69
14	8	38	68
15	7	37	67
16	6	36	66
17	5	35	65
18	4	34	64
19	3	33	63
20	2	32	62
21	1	31	61

LEO BIRTHDAYS

July 23	Max Heindel, Raymond Chandler
July 24	Amelia Earhart, Bella Abzug, Zelda Fitzgerald
July 25	Walter Brennan, Eric Hoffer
July 26	Carl Jung, Stanley Kubrick, Gracie Allen
July 27	Keenan Wynn, Mary Butterworth
July 28	Beatrix Potter, Jacqueline Onassis
July 29	William Powell, Dag Hammarskjold
July 30	Emily Bronte, Elena Blavatsky
July 31	George Baxter, Evonne Goolagong
Aug. 1	Herman Melville, Maria Mitchell
Aug. 2	Myrna Loy, James Baldwin, Helen Morgan
Aug. 3	Dolores Del Rio, Tony Bennett
Aug. 4	Percy Bysshe Shelley
Aug. 5	Neil Armstrong, Clara Bow
Aug. 6	Lucille Ball, Louella Parsons
Aug. 7	Mata Hari, Billie Burke, Anna Magnani
Aug. 8	Andy Warhol, Sylvia Sidney, Esther Williams
Aug. 9	David Steinberg
Aug. 10	Herbert Hoover, Norma Shearer
Aug. 11	Louise Bogan
Aug. 12	Cecil B. DeMille
Aug. 13	Annie Oakley, Lucy Stone
Aug. 14	John Galsworthy, Debbie Meyer
Aug. 15	Napoleon, Julia Child, Edna Ferber
Aug. 16	Ann Blyth, George Meany
Aug. 17	Davy Crockett, Mae West
Aug. 18	Shelley Winters, Virginia Dare
Aug. 19	Orville Wright, Ogden Nash, William J. Clinton
Aug. 20	Van Johnson, Jacquelline Susann
Aug. 21	Count Basie, Princess Margaret
Aug. 22	Debussy, Ray Bradbury, Dorothy Parker
Aug. 23	Louis XVI, Viva

CAN ASTROLOGY PREDICT THE FUTURE?

Can astrology really peer into the future? By studying the planets and the stars is it possible to look years ahead and make predictions for our lives? How can we draw the line between ignorant superstition and cosmic mystery? We live in a very civilized world, to be sure. We consider ourselves modern, enlightened individuals. Yet few of us can resist the temptation to take a peek at the future when we think it's possible. Why? What is the basis of such universal curiosity?

The answer is simple. Astrology works, and you don't have to be a magician to find that out. We certainly can't prove astrology simply by taking a look at the astonishing number of people who believe in it, but such figures do make us wonder what lies behind such widespread popularity. Everywhere in the world hundreds of thousands of serious, intelligent people are charting, studying, and interpreting the positions of the planets and stars every day. Every facet of the media dispenses daily astrological bulletins to millions of curious seekers. In Eastern countries, the source of many wisdoms handed down to us from antiquity, astrology still has a vital place. Why? Surrounded as we are by sophisticated scientific method, how does astrology, with all its bizarre symbolism and mysterious meaning, survive so magnificently? The answer remains the same. It works.

Nobody knows exactly where astrological knowledge came from. We have references to it dating back to the dawn of human history. Wherever there was a stirring of human consciousness, people began to observe the natural cycles and rhythms that sustained their life. The diversity of human behavior must have been evident even to the first students of consciousness. Yet the basic similarity between members of the human family must have led to the search for some common source, some greater point of origin somehow linked to the heavenly bodies ruling our sense of life and time. The ancient world of Mesopotamia, Chaldea, and Egypt was a highly developed center of astronomical observation and astrological interpretation of heavenly phenomena and their resultant effects on human life.

Amid the seeming chaos of a mysterious unknown universe, people from earliest times sought to classify, define, and organize the world around them. Order: that's what the human mind has always striven to maintain in an unceasing battle with its natural counterpart, chaos, or entropy. We build cities, countries, and empires, subjugating nature to a point of near defeat, and then . . . civilization collapses, empires fall, and cities crumble. Nature reclaims the wilderness. Shelly's poem *Ozymandias* is a hymn to the battle between order and chaos. The narrator tells us about a statue, broken, shattered, and half-sunk somewhere in the middle of a distant desert. The inscription reads: "Look on my works, ye mighty, and despair." And then we are told: "Nothing beside remains. Round the decay of that colossal wreck, boundless and bare, the lone and level sands stretch far away."

People always feared the entropy that seemed to lurk in nature. So we found permanence and constancy in the regular movements of the Sun, Moon, and planets and in the positions of the stars. Traditions sprang up from observations of the seasons and crops. Relationships were noted between phenomena in nature and the configurations of the heavenly bodies. This "synchronicity," as it was later called by Carl Jung, extended to thought, mood, and behavior, and as such developed the astrological archetypes handed down to us today.

Astrology, a regal science of the stars in the old days, was made available to the king, who was informed of impending events in the heavens, translated of course to their earthly meanings by trusted astrologers. True, astrological knowledge in its infant stages was rudimentary and beset with many superstitions and false premises. But those same dangers exist today in any investigation of occult or mystical subjects. In the East, reverence for astrology is part of religion. Astrologer-astronomers have held respected positions in government and have taken part in advisory councils on many momentous issues. The duties of the court astrologer, whose office was one of the most important in the land, were clearly defined, as early records show.

Here in our sleek Western world, astrology glimmers on, perhaps more brilliantly than ever. With all of our technological wonders and complex urbanized environments, we look to astrology even now to cut through artificiality, dehumanization, and all the materialism of contemporary life, while we gather precious information that helps us live in that material world. Astrology helps us restore balance and get in step with our own rhythms and the rhythms of nature.

Intelligent investigation of astrology (or the practical application of it) need not mean blind acceptance. We only need to see it working, see our own lives confirming its principles every day, in order to accept and understand it more. To understand ourselves is to know ourselves and to know all. This book can help you to do that—to understand yourself and through understanding develop your own resources and potentials as a rich human being.

YOUR PLACE AMONG THE STARS

Humanity finds itself at the center of a vast personal universe that extends infinitely outward in all directions. In that sense each is a kind of star radiating, as our Sun does, to all bodies everywhere. These vibrations, whether loving, helpful, or destructive, extend outward and generate a kind of "atmosphere" in which woman and man move. The way we relate to everything around us—our joy or our sorrow—becomes a living part of us. Our loved ones and our enemies become the objects of our projected radiations, for better or worse. Our bodies and faces reflect thoughts and emotions much the way light from the Sun reflects the massive reactions occurring deep within its interior. This energy and light reach all who enter its sphere of influence.

Our own personal radiations are just as potent in their own way, really. The reactions that go on deep within us profoundly affect our way of thinking and acting. Our feelings of joy or satisfaction, frustration or anger, must eventually find an outlet. Otherwise we experience the psychological or physiological repercussions of repression. If we can't have a good cry, tell someone our troubles, or express love, we soon feel very bad indeed.

As far as our physical selves are concerned, there is a direct relationship between our outer lives, inner reactions and actions, and the effects on our physical body. We all know the feeling of being startled by the sudden ring of a telephone, or the simple frustration of missing a bus. In fact, our minds and bodies are constantly reacting to outside forces. At the same time we, too, are generating actions that will cause a reaction in someone else. You may suddenly decide to phone a friend. If you are a bus driver you might speed along on your way and leave behind an angry would-be passenger. Whatever the case, mind and body are in close communication and they both reflect each other's condition. Next time you're really angry take a good long look in the mirror!

In terms of human evolution, our ability to understand, control, and ultimately change ourselves will naturally affect all of our outside relationships. Astrology is invaluable to helping us comprehend our inner selves. It is a useful tool in helping us retain our integrity, while cooperating with and living in a world full of other human beings.

Let's go back to our original question: Can astrology predict the future? To know that, we must come to an understanding of what the future is.

In simplest terms the future is the natural next step to the present, just as the present is a natural progression from the past. Although our minds can move from one to the other, there is a thread of continuity between past, present, and future that joins them together in a coherent sequence. If you are reading this book at this moment, it is the result of a real conscious choice you made in the recent past. That is, you chose to find out what was on these pages, picked up the book, and opened it. Because of this choice you may know yourself better in the future. It's as simple as that.

Knowing ourselves is the key to being able to predict and understand our own future. To learn from past experiences, choices, and actions is to fully grasp the present. Coming to grips with the present is to be master of the future.

"Know thyself" is a motto that takes us back to the philosophers of ancient Greece. Mystery religions and cults of initiation throughout the ancient world, schools of mystical discipline, yoga and mental expansion have always been guardians of this one sacred phrase. Know thyself. Of course, that's easy to say. But how do you go about it when there are so many conflicts in our lives and different parts of our personalities? How do we know when we are really "being ourselves" and not merely being influenced by the things we read or see on television, or by the people around us? How can we differentiate the various parts of our character and still remain whole?

There are many methods of classifying human beings into types. Body shapes, muscular types, blood types, and genetic types are only a few. Psychology has its own ways of classifying human beings according to their behavior. Anthropology studies human evolution as the body-mind response to environment. Biology watches physical development and adaptations in body structure. These fields provide valuable information about human beings and the ways they survive, grow, and change in their search for their place in eternity. Yet these branches of science have been separate and fragmented. Their contribution has been to provide theories and data, yes, but no lasting solutions to the human problems that have existed since the first two creatures realized they had two separate identities.

It's often difficult to classify yourself according to these different schemes. It's not easy to be objective about yourself. Some things are hard to face; others are hard to see. The different perspectives afforded to us by studying the human organism from all these different disciplines may seem contradictory when they are all really trying to integrate humankind into the whole of the cosmic scheme.

Astrology can help these disciplines unite to seek a broader and deeper approach to universal human issues. Astrology's point of view is vast. It transcends racial, ethnic, genetic, environmental, and even historical criteria, yet somehow includes them all. Astrology embraces the totality of human experience, then sets about to examine the relationships that are created within that experience.

We don't simply say, "The planets cause this or that." Rather than merely isolating cause or effect, astrology has unified the ideas of cause and effect. Concepts of past, present, and future merge and become, as we shall see a little later on, like stepping-stones across the great stream of mind. Observations of people and the environment have developed the astrological principles of planetary "influence," but it must be remembered that if there is actual influence, it is mutual. As the planets influence us, so we influence them, for we are forever joined to all past and future motion of the heavenly bodies. This is the foundation of astrology as it has been built up over the centuries.

ORDER VS. CHAOS

But is it all written in the stars? Is it destined that empires should thrive and flourish, kings reign, lovers love, and then . . . decay, ruin, and natural disintegration hold sway? Have we anything to do with determining the cycles of order and chaos? The art of the true astrologer depends on his ability to uncover new information, place it upon the grid of data already collected, and then interpret what he sees as accurate probability in human existence. There may be a paradox here. If we can predict that birds will fly south, could we not, with enough time and samples for observation, determine their ultimate fate when they arrive in the south?

The paradox is that there is no paradox at all. Order and chaos exist together simultaneously in one observable universe. At some remote point in time and space the Earth was formed, and for one reason or another, life appeared here. Whether the appearance of life on planets is a usual phenomenon or an unrepeated accident we can only speculate at this moment. But our Earth and all living things upon its surface conform to certain laws of physical materiality that our observations have led us to write down and contemplate. All creatures, from the one-celled ameba to a man hurrying home at rush hour, have some basic traits in common. Life in its organization goes from the simple to the complex with a perfection and order that is both awesome and inspiring. If there were no order to our physical world, an apple could turn into a worm and cows could be butterflies.

But the world is an integrated whole, unified with every other part of creation. When nature does take an unexpected turn, we call that a mutation. This is the exciting card in the program of living experience that tells us not everything is written at all. Spontaneity is real. Change is real. Freedom from the expected norm is real. We have seen in nature that only those mutations that can adapt to changes in their environment and continue reproducing themselves will survive. But possibilities are open for sudden transformation, and that keeps the whole world growing.

FREE CHOICE AND
THE VALUE OF PREDICTIONS

Now it's time to turn our attention to the matter of
predictions. That was our original question after all:
Can astrology peer into the future? Well, astrological
prognostication is an awe-inspiring art and requires
deep philosophical consideration before it is to be un-
dertaken. Not only are there many grids that must be
laid one upon the other before such predictions can be
made, but there are ethical issues that plague every
student of the stars. How much can you really see?
How much should you tell? What is the difference between revealing valuable data and disclosing negative
or harmful programing?

If an astrologer tells you only the good things, you'll
have little confidence in the analysis when you are
passing through crisis. On the other hand, if the astrologer is a prophet of doom who can see nothing but
the dark clouds on the horizon, you will eventually
have to reject astrology because you will come to associate it with the bad luck in your life.

Astrology itself is beyond any practitioner's capacity
to grasp it all. Unrealistic utopianism or gloomy deter-
minism reflect not the truth of astrology but the truth
of the astrologer interpreting what he sees. In order to
solve problems and make accurate predictions, you
have to be *able* to look on the dark side of things without dwelling there. You have to be able to take a look
at all the possibilities, all the possible meanings of a
certain planetary influence without jumping to prema-

ture conclusions. Objective scanning and assessment take much practice and great skill.

No matter how skilled the astrologer is, he cannot assume the responsibility for your life. Only you can take that responsibility as your life unfolds. In a way, the predictions of this book are glancing ahead up the road, much the way a road map can indicate turns up ahead this way or that. You, however, are still driving the car.

What, then, is a horoscope? If it is a picture of you at your moment of birth, are you then frozen forever in time and space, unable to budge or deviate from the harsh, unyielding declarations of the stars? Not at all.

The universe is always in motion. Each moment follows the moment before it. As the present is the result of all past choices and action, so the future is the result of today's choices. But if we can go to a planetary calendar and see where planets will be located two years from now, then how can individual free choice exist? This is a question that has haunted authors and philosophers since the first thinkers recorded their thoughts. In the end, of course, we must all reason things out for ourselves and come to our own conclusions. It is easy to be impressed or influenced by people who seem to know a lot more than we do, but in reality we must all find codes of beliefs with which we are the most comfortable.

But if we can stretch our imaginations up, up above the line of time as it exists from one point to another, we can almost see past, present, and future, all together. We can almost feel this vibrant thread of creative free choice that pushes forward at every moment, actually causing the future to happen! Free will, that force that changes the entire course of a stream, exists within the stream of mind itself—the collective mind, or intelligence, of humanity. Past, present, and future are mere stepping-stones across that great current.

Our lives continue a thread of an intelligent mind

that existed before we were born and will exist after we die. It is like an endless relay race. At birth we pick up a torch and carry it, lighting the way with that miraculous light of consciousness of immortality. Then we pass it on to others when we die. What we call the *unconscious* may be part of this great stream of mind, which learns and shares experiences with everything that has ever lived or will ever live on this world or any other.

Yet we all come to Earth with different family circumstances, backgrounds, and characteristics. We all come to life with different planetary configurations. Indeed each person *is* different, yet we are all the same. We have different tasks or responsibilities or lifestyles, but underneath we share a common current—the powerful stream of human intelligence. Each of us has different sets of circumstances to deal with because of the choices he or she has made in the past. We all possess different assets and have different resources to fall back on, weaknesses to strengthen, and sides of our nature to transform. We are all what we are now because of what we were before. The present is the sum of the past. And we will be what we will be in the future because of what we are now.

It is foolish to pretend that there are no specific boundaries or limitations to any of our particular lives. Family background, racial, cultural, or religious indoctrinations, physical characteristics, these are all inescapable facts of our being that must be incorporated and accepted into our maturing mind. But each person possesses the capacity for breakthrough, forgiveness, and total transformation. It has taken millions of years since people first began to walk upright. We cannot expect an overnight evolution to take place. There are many things about our personalities that are very much like our parents. Sometimes that thought makes us uncomfortable, but it's true.

It's also true that we are not our parents. You are

you, just you, and nobody else but you. That's one of the wondrous aspects of astrology. The levels on which each planetary configuration works out will vary from individual to individual. Often an aspect of selfishness will be manifested in one person, yet in another it may appear as sacrifice and kindness.

Development is inevitable in human consciousness. But the direction of that development is not. As plants will bend toward the light as they grow, so there is the possibility for the human mind to grow toward the light of integrity and truth. The Age of Aquarius that everyone is talking about must first take place within each human's mind and heart. An era of peace, freedom, and community cannot be legislated by any government, no matter how liberal. It has to be a spontaneous flow of human spirit and fellowship. It will be a magnificent dawning on the globe of consciousness that reflects the joy of the human heart to be part of the great stream of intelligence and love. It must be generated by an enlightened, realistic humanity. There's no law that can put it into effect, no magic potion to drink that will make it all come true. It will be the result of all people's efforts to assume their personal and social responsibilities and to carve out a new destiny for humankind.

As you read the predictions in this book, bear in mind that they have been calculated by means of planetary positions for whole groups of people. Thus their value lies in your ability to coordinate what you read with the nature of your life's circumstances at the present time. You have seen how many complex relationships must be analyzed in individual horoscopes before sensible accurate conclusions can be drawn. No matter what the indications, a person has his or her own life, own intelligence, basic native strength that must ultimately be the source of action and purpose. When you are living truthfully and in harmony with what you know is right, there are no forces, threats, or obstacles that can defeat you.

With these predictions, read the overall pattern and see how rhythms begin to emerge. They are not caused by remote alien forces, millions of miles out in space. You and the planets are one. What you do, they do. What they do, you do. But can you change their course? No, but you cannot change many of your basic characteristics either. Still, within that already existing framework, you are the master. You can still differentiate between what is right for you and what is not. You can seize opportunities and act on them, you can create beauty and seek love.

The purpose of looking ahead is not to scare yourself. Look ahead to enlarge your perspective, enhance your overall view of the life *you* are developing. Difficult periods cause stress certainly, but at the same time they give you the chance to reassess your condition, restate and redefine exactly what is important to you, so you can cherish your life more. Joyous periods should be lived to the fullest with the happiness and exuberance that each person richly deserves.

YOUR HOROSCOPE AND THE ZODIAC

It's possible that in your own body, as you read this passage, there exist atoms as old as time itself. You could well be the proud possessor of some carbon and hydrogen (two necessary elements in the development of life) that came into being in the heart of a star billions and billions of years ago. That star could have exploded and cast its matter far into space. This matter could have formed another star, and then another, until finally our Sun was born. From the Sun's nuclear reactions came the material that later formed the planets—and maybe some of that primeval carbon or hydrogen. That material could have become part of the Earth, part of an early ocean, even early life. These same atoms could well have been carried down to the present day, to this very moment as you read this book. It's really quite possible. You can see how everything is linked to everything else. Our Earth now exists in a gigantic universe that showers it constantly with rays and invisible particles. You are the point into which all these energies and influences have been focused. You are the prism through which all the light of outer space is being refracted. You are literally a reflection of all the planets and stars.

Your horoscope is a picture of the sky at the moment of your birth. It's like a gigantic snapshot of the positions of the planets and stars, taken from Earth. Of course, the planets never stop moving around the Sun even for the briefest moment, and you represent that motion as it was occurring at the exact hour of your birth at the precise location on the Earth where you were born.

When an astrologer is going to read your chart, he or she asks you for the month, day, and year of your birth. She also needs the exact time and place. With this information he sets about consulting various charts and tables in his calculation of the specific positions of the Sun, Moon, and stars, relative to your birthplace when you came to Earth. Then he or she locates them by means of the *Zodiac*.

The Zodiac is a group of stars, centered against the Sun's apparent path around the Earth, and these star groups are divided into twelve equal segments, or *signs*. What we are actually dividing up is the Earth's path around the Sun. But from our point of view here on Earth, it seems as if the Sun is making a great circle around our planet in the sky, so we say it's the Sun's apparent path. This twelvefold division, the Zodiac, is like a mammoth address system for any body in the sky. At any given moment, the planets can all be located at a specific point along this path.

Now where are you in this system? First you look to your *Sun sign*—the section of the Zodiac that the Sun occupied when you were born. A great part of your character, in fact the central thread of your whole being, is described by your Sun sign. Each sign of the Zodiac has certain basic traits associated with it. Since the Sun remains in each sign for about thirty days, that divides the population into twelve major character types. Of course, not everybody born the same month will have the same character, but you'll be amazed at how many fundamental traits you share with your astrological cousins of the same birth sign, no matter how many environmental differences you boast.

The dates on which the Sun sign changes will vary from year to year. That is why some people born near the *cusp*, or edge, of a sign have difficulty determining their true birth sign without the aid of an astrologer who can plot precisely the Sun's apparent motion (the Earth's motion) for any given year. But to help you find your true Sun sign, a Table of Cusp Dates for the years 1900 to 2010 is provided for you on page 17.

Here are the twelve signs of the Zodiac as western astrology has recorded them. Listed also are the symbols associated with them and the *approximate* dates when the Sun enters and exits each sign for the year 2003.

Aries	Ram	March 20–April 20
Taurus	Bull	April 20–May 21
Gemini	Twins	May 21–June 21
Cancer	Crab	June 21–July 23
Leo	Lion	July 23–August 23
Virgo	Virgin	August 23–September 23
Libra	Scales	September 23–October 23
Scorpio	Scorpion	October 23–November 22
Sagittarius	Archer	November 22–December 22
Capricorn	Sea Goat	December 22–January 20
Aquarius	Water Bearer	January 20–February 18
Pisces	Fish	February 18–March 20

In a horoscope the *Rising sign*, or Ascendant, is often considered to be as important as the Sun sign. In a later chapter (see pages 82–84) the Rising sign is discussed in detail. But to help you determine your own Rising sign, a Table of Rising Signs is provided for you on pages 20–21.

THE SIGNS OF THE ZODIAC

The signs of the Zodiac are an ingenious and complex summary of human behavioral and physical types, handed down from generation to generation through the bodies of all people in their hereditary material and through their minds. On the following pages you will find brief descriptions of all twelve signs in their highest and most ideal expression.

ARIES
The Sign of the Ram

Aries is the first sign of the Zodiac, and marks the beginning of springtime and the birth of the year. In spring the Earth begins its ascent upward and tips its North Pole toward the Sun. During this time the life-giving force of the Sun streams toward Earth, bathing our planet with the kiss of warmth and life. Plants start growing. Life wakes up. No more waiting. No more patience. The message has come from the Sun: Time to live!

Aries is the sign of the Self and is the crusade for the right of an individual to live in unimpeachable freedom. It represents the supremacy of the human will over all obstacles, limitations, and threats. In Aries there is unlimited energy, optimism, and daring, for it is the pioneer in search of a new world. It is the story of success and renewal, championship, and victory. It is the living spirit of resilience and the power to be yourself, free from all restrictions and conditioning. There is no pattern you *have* to repeat, nobody's rule you *have* to follow.

Confidence and positive action are born in Aries, with little thought or fear of the past. Life is as magic as sunrise, with all the creative potential ahead of you for a new day. Activity, energy, and adventure characterize this sign. In this sector of the Zodiac there is amazing strength, forthrightness, honesty, and a stubborn refusal to accept defeat. The Aries nature is forgiving, persuasive, masterful, and decisive.

In short, Aries is the magic spark of life and being, the source of all initiative, courage, independence, and self-esteem.

TAURUS
The Sign of the Bull

Taurus is wealth. It is not just money, property, and the richness of material possessions, but also a wealth of the spirit. Taurus rules everything in the visible world we see, touch, hear, smell, taste—the Earth, sea, and sky—everything we normally consider "real." It is the sign of economy and reserve, for it is a mixture of thrift and luxury, generosity and practicality. It is a blend of the spiritual and material, for the fertility of the sign is unlimited, and in this sense it is the mystical bank of life. Yet it must hold the fruit of its efforts in its hands and seeks to realize its fantasy-rich imagination with tangible rewards.

Loyalty and endurance make this sign perhaps the most stable of all. We can lean on Taurus, count on it,

and it makes our earthly lives comfortable, safe, pleasurable. It is warm, sensitive, loving, and capable of
magnificent, joyful sensations. It is conservative and
pragmatic, with a need to be sure of each step forward.
It is the capacity to plan around eventualities without
living in the future. Steadfast and constant, this is a
sturdy combination of ruggedness and beauty, gentle-
ness and unshakability of purpose. It is the point at
which we join body and soul. Unselfish friend and loyal
companion, Taurus is profoundly noble and openly humanitarian. Tenacity and concentration slow the energy down to bring certain long-lasting rewards.

Taurus is a fertile resource and rich ground to grow in,
and we all need it for our ideas and plans to flourish. It is
the uncut diamond, symbolizing rich, raw tastes and a
deep need for satisfaction, refinement, and completion.

GEMINI
The Sign of the Twins

Gemini is the sign of mental brilliance. Communication
is developed to a high degree of fluidity, rapidity, fluency.
It is the chance for expressing ideas and relaying information from one place to another. Charming, debonair,
and lighthearted, it is a symbol of universal interest and
eternal curiosity. The mind is quick and advanced, with a
lightning-like ability to assimilate data.

It is the successful manipulation of verbal or visual
language and the capacity to meet all events with ob-
jectivity and intelligence. It is light, quick wit, with a
comic satiric twist. Gemini is the sign of writing or
speaking.

Gemini is the willingness to try anything once, a need to wander and explore, the quick shifting of moods and attitudes being a basic characteristic that indicates a need for change. Versatility is the remarkable Gemini attribute. It is the capacity to investigate, perform, and relate over great areas for short periods of time and thus to connect all areas. It is mastery of design and perception, the power to conceptualize and create by putting elements together—people, colors, patterns. It is the reporter's mind, plus a brilliant ability to see things in objective, colorful arrangement. Strength lies in constant refreshment of outlook and joyful participation in all aspects of life.

Gemini is involvement with neighbors, family and relatives, telephones, arteries of news and communication—anything that enhances the human capacity for communication and self-expression. It is active, positive, and energetic, with an insatiable hunger for human interchange. Through Gemini bright and dark sides of personality merge and the mind has wings. As it flies it reflects the light of a boundless shining intellect. It is the development of varied talents from recognition of the duality of self.

Gemini is geared toward enjoying life to the fullest by finding, above all else, a means of expressing the inner self to the outside world.

CANCER
The Sign of the Crab

Cancer is the special relationship to home and involvement with the family unit. Maintaining harmony in the domestic sphere or improving conditions there is a major characteristic in this sector of the Zodiac. Cancer is attachment between two beings vibrating in sympathy with one another.

It is the comfort of a loving embrace, a tender generosity. Cancer is the place of shelter whenever there are lost or hungry souls in the night. Through Cancer we are fed, protected, comforted, and soothed. When the coldness of the world threatens, Cancer is there with gentle understanding. It is protection and understated loyalty, a medium of rich, living feeling that is both psychic and mystical. Highly intuitive, Cancer has knowledge that other signs do not possess. It is the wisdom of the soul.

It prefers the quiet contentment of the home and hearth to the busy search for earthly success and civilized pleasures. Still, there is a respect for worldly knowledge. Celebration of life comes through food. The sign is the muted light of warmth, security, and gladness, and its presence means nourishment. It rules fertility and the instinct to populate and raise young. It is growth of the soul. It is the ebb and flow of all our tides of feeling, involvements, habits, and customs.

Through Cancer is reflected the inner condition of all human beings, and therein lies the seed of knowledge out of which the soul will grow.

LEO
The Sign of the Lion

Leo is love. It represents the warmth, strength, and regeneration we feel through love. It is the radiance of life-giving light and the center of all attention and activity. It is passion, romance, adventure, and games. Pleasure, amusement, fun, and entertainment are all part of Leo. Based on the capacity for creative feeling and the desire to express love, Leo is the premier sign. It represents the unlimited outpouring of all that is warm and positive.

It is loyalty, dignity, responsibility, and command. Pride and nobility belong to Leo, and the dashing image of the knight in shining armor, of the hero, is part of Leo. It is a sense of high honor and kingly generosity born out of deep, noble love. It is the excitement of the sportsman, with all the unbeatable flair and style of success. It is a strong, unyielding will and true sense of personal justice, a respect for human freedom, and an enlightened awareness of people's needs.

Leo is involvement in the Self's awareness of personal talents and the desire and need to express them. At best it is forthrightness, courage and efficiency, authority and dignity, showmanship, and a talent for organization. Dependable and ardent, the Lion is characterized by individuality, positivism, and integrity.

It is the embodiment of human maturity, the effective individual in society, a virile creative force able to take chances and win. It is the love of laughter and the joy of making others happy. Decisive and enthusiastic, the Lion is the creative producer of the Zodiac It is the potential to light the way for others.

VIRGO
The Sign of the Virgin

Virgo is the sign of work and service. It is the symbol of the farmer at harvest time, and represents tireless efforts for the benefit of humanity, the joy of bringing the fruits of the Earth to the table of mankind. Celebration through work is the characteristic of this sign.

Sincerity, zeal, discipline, and devotion mark the sign of the Virgin.

The key word is purity, and in Virgo lies a potential for unlimited self-mastery. Virgo is the embodiment of perfected skill and refined talent. The thread of work is woven into the entire life of Virgo. All creativity is poured into streamlining a job, classifying a system, eradicating unnecessary elements of pure analysis. The true Virgo genius is found in separating the wheat from the chaff.

Spartan simplicity characterizes this sign, and Virgo battles the war between order and disorder. The need to arrange, assimilate, and categorize is great; it is the symbol of the diagnostician, the nurse, and the healer. Criticism and analysis describe this sign—pure, incisive wisdom and a shy appreciation of life's joys. All is devoted to the attainment of perfection and the ideal of self-mastery.

Virgo is the sign of health and represents the physical body as a functioning symbol of the mental and spiritual planes. It is the state of healing the ills of the human being with natural, temperate living. It is maturation of the ego as it passes from a self-centered phase to its awareness and devotion to humanity.

It is humanitarian, pragmatic, and scientific, with boundless curiosity. Focus and clarity of mind are the strong points, while strength of purpose and shy reserve underlie the whole sign. There is separateness, aloofness, and solitude for this beacon of the Zodiac. As a lighthouse guides ships, so Virgo shines.

LIBRA
The Sign of the Scales

Libra is the sign of human relationship, marriage, equality, and justice. It symbolizes the need of one human being for another, the capacity to find light, warmth, and life-giving love in relationship to another human being. It is union on any level—mental, sexual, emotional, or business. It is self-extension in a desire to find a partner with whom to share our joys. It is the capacity to recognize the needs of others and to develop to the fullest our powers of diplomacy, good taste, and refinement.

Libra is harmony, grace, aesthetic sensibility, and the personification of the spirit of companionship. It represents the skill to maintain balances and the ability to share mutually all life's benefits, trials, crises, and blessings. Libra is mastery at anticipation of another's needs or reactions. It is the exercise of simple justice with impartial delicacy.

It is the need to relate, to find a major person, place, or thing to sustain us and draw out our attention. It is growth through becoming awakened to the outside world and other people. It is the union of two loving souls in honesty, equality, mutual cooperation, and mutual accord.

SCORPIO
The Sign of the Scorpion

Scorpio is the sign of dark intensity, swirling passion, and sexual magnetism. It is the thirst for survival and regeneration that are the bases of sexual orientation and the creative impulses for self-expression. No other sign has such a profound instinct for survival and reproduction. Out of the abyss of emotions come a thousand creations, each one possessing a life of its own.

Scorpio is completion, determination, and endurance, fortified with enough stamina to outlive any enemy. It is the pursuit of goals despite any threat, warning, or obstacle that might stand in the way. It simply cannot be stopped. It knows when to wait and when to proceed. It is the constant state of readiness, a vibrant living force that constantly pumps out its rhythm from the depths of being.

Secretive and intimate, Scorpio symbolizes the self-directed creature with a will of steel. It is the flaming desire to create, manipulate, and control with a magician's touch. But the most mysterious quality is the capacity for metamorphosis, or total transformation.

This represents supremacy in the battle with dark unseen forces. It is the state of being totally fearless—the embodiment of truth and courage. It symbolizes the human capacity to face all danger and emerge supreme, to heal oneself. As a caterpillar spins its way into the darkness of a cocoon, Scorpio faces the end of existence, says goodbye to an old way of life, and goes through a kind of death—or total change.

Then, amid the dread of uncertainty, something remarkable happens. From hopelessness or personal crisis a new individual emerges, like a magnificent butterfly leaving behind its cocoon. It is a human being completely transformed and victorious. This is Scorpio.

SAGITTARIUS
The Sign of the Archer

Sagittarius is the sign of adventure and a thousand and one new experiences. It is the cause and purpose of every new attempt at adventure or self-understanding. It is the embodiment of enthusiasm, search for truth, and love of wisdom. Hope and optimism characterize this section of the Zodiac, and it is the ability to leave the past behind and set out again with positive resilience and a happy, cheerful outlook.

It is intelligence and exuberance, youthful idealism, and the desire to expand all horizons. It is the constant hatching of dreams, the hunger for knowledge, travel and experience. The goal is exploration itself.

Sagittarius is generosity, humor, and goodness of nature, backed up by the momentum of great expectations. It symbolizes the ability of people to be back in the race after having the most serious spills over the biggest hurdles. It is a healthy, positive outlook and the capacity to meet each new moment with unaffected buoyancy.

At this point in the Zodiac, greater conscious understanding begins to develop self-awareness and self-acceptance. It is an Olympian capacity to look upon the bright side and to evolve that aspect of mind we call conscience.

CAPRICORN
The Sign of the Sea Goat

Capricorn is the sign of structure and physical law. It rules depth, focus, and concentration. It is the symbol of success through perseverance, happiness through profundity. It is victory over disruption, and finds reality in codes set up by society and culture. It is the perpetuation of useful, tested patterns and a desire to protect what has already been established.

It is cautious, conservative, conscious of the passage of time, yet ageless. The Goat symbolizes the incorporation of reason into living and depth into loving.

Stability, responsibility, and fruitfulness through loyalty color this sector of the Zodiac with an undeniable and irrepressible awareness of success, reputation, and honor. Capricorn is the culmination of our earthly dreams, the pinnacle of our worldly life.

It is introspection and enlightenment through serious contemplation of the Self and its position in the world. It is mastery of understanding and the realization of dreams.

Capricorn is a winter blossom, a born professional with an aim of harmony and justice, beauty, grace, and success. It is the well-constructed pyramid: perfect and beautiful, architecturally correct, mysteriously implacable, and hard to know. It is highly organized and built on precise foundations to last and last and last. It is practical, useful yet magnificent and dignified, signifying permanence and careful planning. Like a pyramid, Capricorn has thick impenetrable walls, complex passageways, and false corridors. Yet somewhere at the heart of this ordered structure is the spirit of a mighty ruler.

AQUARIUS
The Sign of the Water Bearer

Aquarius is the symbol of idealized free society. It is the herding instinct in man as a social animal. It is the collection of heterogeneous elements of human consciousness in coherent peaceful coexistence. Friendship, goodwill, and harmonious contact are Aquarius attributes. It is founded on the principle of individual freedom and the brotherly love and respect for the rights of all men and women on Earth.

It is strength of will and purpose, altruism, and love of human fellowship. It is the belief in spontaneity and free choice, in the openness to live in a spirit of harmony and cooperation—liberated from restriction, repression, and conventional codes of conduct. It is the brilliant capacity to assimilate information instantaneously at the last minute and translate that information into immediate creative action, and so the result is to live in unpredictability.

This is the progressive mind, the collective mind—groups of people getting together to celebrate life. Aquarius is the child of the future, the utopian working for the betterment of the human race. Funds, charities, seeking better cities and better living conditions for others, involvement in great forms of media or communication, science or research in the hope of joining mankind to his higher self—this is all Aquarius.

It is invention, genius, revolution, discovery—instantaneous breakthrough from limitations. It's a departure from convention, eccentricity, the unexpected development that changes the course of history. It is the discovery of people and all the arteries that join them together. Aquarius is adventure, curiosity, exotic and alien appeal. It pours the water of life and intelligence for all humanity to drink. It is humanism, community, and the element of surprise.

PISCES
The Sign of the Fishes

Pisces is faith—undistracted, patient, all-forgiving faith—and therein lies the Pisces capacity for discipline, endurance, and stamina.

It is imagination and other-worldliness, the condition

of living a foggy, uncertain realm of poetry, music, and fantasy. Passive and compassionate, this sector of the Zodiac symbolizes the belief in the inevitability of life. It represents the view of life that everything exists in waves, like the sea. All reality as we know it is a dream, a magic illusion that must ultimately be washed away. Tides pull this way and that, whirlpools and undercurrents sweep across the bottom of life's existence, but in Pisces there is total acceptance of all tides, all rhythms, all possibilities. It is the final resolution of all personal contradictions and all confusing paradoxes.

It is the search for truth and honesty, and the devotion to love, utterly and unquestionably. It is the desire to act with wisdom, kindness, and responsibility and to welcome humanity completely free from scorn, malice, discrimination, or prejudice. It is total, all-embracing, idealistic love. It is the acceptance of two sides of a question at once and love through sacrifice.

Pisces is beyond reality. We are here today, but may be gone tomorrow. Let the tide of circumstances carry you where it will, for nothing is forever. As all things come, so must they go. In the final reel, all things must pass away. It is deliverance from sorrow through surrender to the infinite. The emotions are as vast as the ocean, yet in the pain of confusion there is hope in the secret cell of one's own heart. Pisces symbolizes liberation from pain through love, faith, and forgiveness.

THE SIGNS AND
THEIR KEY WORDS

		Positive	Negative
ARIES	self	courage, initiative, pioneer instinct	brash rudeness, selfish impetuosity
TAURUS	money	endurance, loyalty, wealth	obstinacy, gluttony
GEMINI	mind	versatility, communication	capriciousness, unreliability
CANCER	family	sympathy, homing instinct	clannishness, childishness
LEO	children	love, authority, integrity	egotism, force
VIRGO	work	purity, industry, analysis	faultfinding, cynicism
LIBRA	marriage	harmony, justice	vacillation, superficiality
SCORPIO	sex	survival, regeneration	vengeance, discord
SAGITTARIUS	travel	optimism, higher learning	lawlessness, irresponsibility
CAPRICORN	career	depth, responsibility	narrowness, gloom
AQUARIUS	friends	humanity, genius	perverse unpredictability
PISCES	faith	spiritual love, universality	diffusion, escapism

THE ELEMENTS AND
THE QUALITIES OF THE SIGNS

Every sign has both an element and a quality associated with it. The element indicates the basic makeup of the sign, and the quality describes the kind of activity associated with each.

Element	Sign	Quality	Sign
Fire	Aries Leo Sagittarius	Cardinal	Aries Libra Cancer Capricorn
Earth	Taurus Virgo Capricorn	Fixed	Taurus Leo Scorpio Aquarius
Air	Gemini Libra Aquarius	Mutable	Gemini Virgo Sagittarius Pisces
Water	Cancer Scorpio Pisces		

Signs can be grouped together according to their element and quality. Signs of the same element share many basic traits in common. They tend to form stable configurations and ultimately harmonious relationships. Signs of the same quality are often less harmonious, but share many dynamic potentials for growth and profound fulfillment.

The following pages describe these sign groupings in more detail.

The Fire Signs

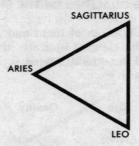

This is the fire group. On the whole these are emotional, volatile types, quick to anger, quick to forgive. They are adventurous, powerful people and act as a source of inspiration for everyone. They spark into action with immediate exuberant impulses. They are intelligent, self-involved, creative, and idealistic. They all share a certain vibrancy and glow that outwardly reflects an inner flame and passion for living.

The Earth Signs

This is the earth group. They are in constant touch with the material world and tend to be conservative. Although they are all capable of spartan self-discipline, they are earthy, sensual people who are stimulated by the tangible, elegant, and luxurious. The thread of their lives is always practical, but they do fantasize and are often attracted to dark, mysterious, emotional people. They are like great cliffs overhanging the sea, forever married to the ocean but always resisting erosion from the dark, emotional forces that thunder at their feet.

The Air Signs

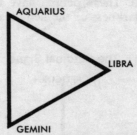

This is the air group. They are light, mental creatures desirous of contact, communication, and relationship. They are involved with people and the forming of ties on many levels. Original thinkers, they are the bearers of human news. Their language is their sense of word, color, style, and beauty. They provide an atmosphere suitable and pleasant for living. They add change and versatility to the scene, and it is through them that we can explore human intelligence and experience.

The Water Signs

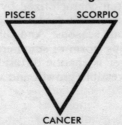

This is the water group. Through the water people, we are all joined together on emotional, nonverbal levels.

The water signs are silent, mysterious types whose magic hypnotizes even the most determined realist. They have uncanny perceptions about people and are as rich as the oceans when it comes to feeling, emotion, or imagination. They are sensitive, mystical creatures with memories that go back beyond time. Through water, life is sustained. These people have the potential for the depths of darkness or the heights of mysticism and art.

The Cardinal Signs

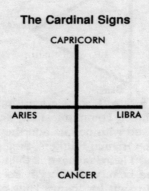

The cardinal signs present a picture of dynamism, activity, tremendous stress, and remarkable achievement. These people know the meaning of great change since their lives are often characterized by significant crises and major successes. The cardinal signs mark the beginning of the four seasons. And this combination is like a simultaneous storm of summer, fall, winter, and spring. The danger is chaotic diffusion of energy; the potential is irrepressible growth and victory.

The Fixed Signs

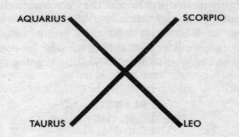

Fixed signs are always establishing themselves in a given place or area of experience. Like explorers who arrive and plant a flag, these people claim a position from which they do not enjoy being deposed. They are staunch, stalwart, upright, trusty, honorable people, although their obstinacy is well-known. Their contribution is fixity, and they are the angels who support our visible world.

The Mutable Signs

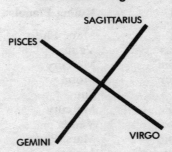

Mutable people are versatile, sensitive, intelligent, nervous, and deeply curious about life. They are the translators of all energy. They often carry out or complete tasks initiated by others. People from mutable signs have highly developed minds; they are imaginative and jumpy and think and talk a lot. At worst their lives are a Tower of Babel. At best they are adaptable and ready creatures who can assimilate one kind of experience and enjoy it while anticipating coming changes.

THE PLANETS AND
THE SIGNS THEY RULE

The signs of the Zodiac are linked to the planets in the following way. Each sign is governed or ruled by one or more planets. No matter where the planets are located in the sky at any given moment, they still rule their respective signs. When they travel through the signs they rule, they have special dignity and their effects are stronger.

Following is a list of the planets and the signs they rule. After you read the definitions of the planets from pages 88 to 96, see if you can determine how the planet ruling *your* Sun sign has affected your life.

Signs	Ruling Planets
Aries	Mars, Pluto
Taurus	Venus
Gemini	Mercury
Cancer	Moon
Leo	Sun
Virgo	Mercury
Libra	Venus
Scorpio	Mars, Pluto
Sagittarius	Jupiter
Capricorn	Saturn
Aquarius	Saturn, Uranus
Pisces	Jupiter, Neptune

THE ZODIAC AND
THE HUMAN BODY

The signs of the Zodiac are linked to the human body in a direct relationship. Each sign has a part of the body with which it is associated.

It is traditionally believed that surgery is best performed when the Moon is passing through a sign *other* than the sign associated with the part of the body upon which an operation is to be performed. But often the presence of the Moon in a particular sign will bring the focus of attention to that very part of the body under medical scrutiny.

The principles of medical astrology are complex and beyond the scope of this introduction. We can, however, list the signs of the Zodiac and the parts of the human body connected with them. Once you learn these correspondences, you'll be amazed at how accurate they are.

Signs	Human Body
Aries	Head, brain, face, upper jaw
Taurus	Throat, neck, lower jaw
Gemini	Hands, arms, lungs, nerves
Cancer	Stomach, breasts, womb, liver
Leo	Heart, spine
Virgo	Intestines, liver
Libra	Kidneys, lower back
Scorpio	Sex and eliminative organs
Sagittarius	Hips, thighs, liver
Capricorn	Skin, bones, teeth, knees
Aquarius	Circulatory system, lower legs
Pisces	Feet, tone of being

THE ZODIACAL HOUSES
AND THE RISING SIGN

Apart from the month and day of birth, the exact time of birth is another vital factor in the determination of an accurate horoscope. Not only do planets move with great speed, but one must know how far the Earth has turned during the day. That way you can determine exactly where the planets are located with respect to the precise birthplace of an individual. This makes your horoscope *your* horoscope.

The horoscope sets up a kind of framework around which the life of an individual grows like wild ivy, this way and that, weaving its way around the trellis of the natal positions of the planets. The year of birth tells us the positions of the distant, slow-moving planets Jupiter, Saturn, Uranus, Neptune, and Pluto. The month of birth indicates the Sun sign, or birth sign as it is commonly called, as well as indicating the positions of the rapidly moving planets Venus, Mercury, and Mars. The day of birth, as well as the time, locates the position of our Moon. And the moment of birth—the exact hour and minute—determines the houses through what is called the Ascendant, or Rising sign.

The illustration on the next page shows the flat chart, or natural wheel, an astrologer uses. The inner circle of the wheel is labeled 1 through 12. These 12 divisions are known as the houses of the Zodiac.

The 1st house always starts from the position marked E, which corresponds to the eastern horizon. The rest of the houses 2 through 12 follow around in a "counterclockwise" direction. The point where each house starts is known as a cusp, or edge.

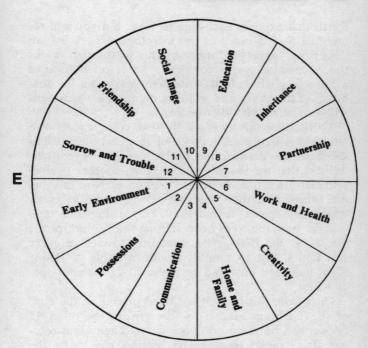

The 12 Houses of the Zodiac

The cusp, or edge, of the 1st house (point E) is where an astrologer would place your Rising sign, the Ascendant. The Rising sign is very important in a horoscope, as it defines your self-image, outlook, physical constitution, early environment, and whole orientation to life. And, as already mentioned, the exact time of your birth determines your Rising sign. Let's see how this works.

As the Earth rotates on its axis once every 24 hours, each one of the 12 signs of the Zodiac appears to be "rising" on the horizon, with a new one appearing about every two hours. Actually it is the turning of the

Earth that exposes each sign to view, but you will remember that in much of our astrological work we are discussing "apparent" motion. This Rising sign marks the Ascendant, and it colors the whole orientation of a horoscope. It indicates the sign governing the first house of the chart, and will thus determine which signs will govern all the other houses.

To visualize this idea, imagine two color wheels with twelve divisions superimposed upon each other. Just as the Zodiac is divided into twelve star groups (constellations) that we identify as the signs, another twelve-fold division is used to denote the houses. Now imagine one wheel (the signs) moving slowly while the other wheel (the houses) remains still. This analogy may help you see how the signs keep shifting the "color" of the houses as the Rising sign continues to change every two hours. But to simplify things, a Table of Rising Signs has been provided on pages 20–21 for your specific Sun sign.

Once your Rising sign has been placed on the cusp of the 1st house, the signs that govern the other 11 houses can be placed on your chart. Then an astrologer, using tables of planetary motion, can locate the positions of all the planets in their appropriate houses. The house where your Sun sign is describes your basic character and your fundamental drives. And the houses where the other planets are in your chart suggest the areas of life on Earth in which you will be most likely to focus your constant energy and center your activity.

The illustration on page 83 briefly identifies each of the 12 houses of the Zodiac. Now the pages that follow provide a detailed discussion of the meanings of the houses. In the section after the houses we will define all the known planets of the solar system, with a separate section on the Moon, in order to acquaint you with more of the astrological vocabulary you will be meeting again and again.

THE MEANING OF THE HOUSES

The twelve houses of every horoscope represent areas of life on Earth, or regions of worldly experience. Depending on which sign of the Zodiac was rising on the eastern horizon at the moment of birth, the activity of each house will be "colored" by the zodiacal sign on its cusp, or edge. In other words, the sign falling on the first house will determine what signs will fall on the rest of the houses.

1 The first house determines the basic orientation to all of life on Earth. It indicates the body type, face, head, and brain. It rules your self-image, or the way others see you because of the way you see your self. This is the Ascendant of the horoscope and is the focus of energies of your whole chart. It acts like a prism through which all of the planetary light passes and is reflected in your life. It colors your outlook and influences everything you do and see.

2 This is the house of finances. Here is your approach to money and materialism in general. It indicates where the best sources are for you to improve your financial condition and your earning power as a whole. It indicates chances for gain or loss. It describes your values, alliances, and assets.

3 This is the house of the day-to-day mind. Short trips, communication, and transportation are associated with this house. It deals with routines, brothers and sisters, relatives, neighbors, and the near environment at hand. Language, letters, and the tools for transmitting information are included in third-house matters.

4 This is the house that describes your home and home life, parents, and childhood in the sense of indicating the kind of roots you come from. It symbolizes your present home and domestic situation and reflects your need for privacy and retreat from the world, indicating, of course, what kind of scene you require.

5 Pleasure, love affairs, amusements, parties, creativity, children. This is the house of passion and courtship and of expressing your talents, whatever they are. It is related to the development of your personal life and the capacity to express feeling and enjoy romance.

6 This is the house of work. Here there are tasks to be accomplished and maladjustments to be corrected. It is the house of health as well, and describes some of the likely places where physical health difficulties may appear. It rules routines, regimen, necessary jobs as opposed to a chosen career, army, navy, police—people employed, co-workers, and those in service to others. It indicates the individual's ability to harvest the fruit of his own efforts.

7 This is the house of marriage, partnership, and unions. It represents the alter ego, all people other than yourself, open confrontation with the public. It describes your partner and the condition of partnership as you discern it. In short, it is your "take" on the world. It indicates your capacity to make the transition from courtship to marriage and specifically what you seek out in others.

8 This is the house of deep personal transition, sex as a form of mutual surrender and interchange between human beings. It is the release from tensions and the completion of the creative processes. The eighth house also has to do with taxes, inheritances, and the finances of others, as well as death as the ending of cycles and crises.

9   This is the house of the higher mind, philosophy, religion, and the expression of personal conscience through moral codes. It indicates political leanings, ethical views, and the capacity of the individual for a broader perspective and deeper understanding of himself in relation to society. It is through the ninth house that you make great strides in learning and travel to distant places and come to know yourself through study, dreams, and wide experience.

10   This is the house of career, honor, and prestige. It marks the culmination of worldly experience and indicates the highest point you can reach, what you look up to, and how high you can go in this lifetime. It describes your parents, employers, and how you view authority figures, the condition and direction of your profession, and your position in the community.

11   This is the house of friendships. It describes your social behavior, your views on humanity, and your hopes, aspirations, and wishes for an ideal life. It will indicate what kinds of groups, clubs, organizations, and friendships you tend to form and what you seek out in your chosen alliances other than with your mate or siblings. This house suggests the capacity for the freedom and unconventionality that an individual is seeking, his sense of his connection with mankind, and the definition of his goals, personal and social.

12   This is the house of seclusion, secret wisdom, and self-incarceration. It indicates our secret enemies as well, in the sense that there may be persons, feelings, or memories we are trying to escape. It is self-undoing in that this house acts against the ego in order to find a higher, more universal purpose. It rules prisons, hospitals, charities, and selfless service. It is the house of unfinished psychic business.

THE PLANETS OF THE SOLAR SYSTEM

The planets of the solar system all travel around the Sun at different speeds and different distances. Taken with the Sun, they all distribute individual intelligence and ability throughout the entire chart.

The planets modify the influence of the Sun in a chart according to their own particular natures, strengths, and positions. Their positions must be calculated for each year and day, and their function and expression in a horoscope will change as they move from one area of the Zodiac to another.

Following, you will find brief statements of their pure meanings.

THE SUN

The Sun is the center of existence. Around this flaming sphere all the planets revolve in endless orbits. Our star is constantly sending out its beams of light and energy without which no life on Earth would be possible. In astrology it symbolizes everything we are trying to become, the center around which all of our activity in life will always revolve. It is the symbol of our basic nature and describes the natural and constant thread that runs through everything that we do from birth to death on this planet.

Everything in the horoscope ultimately revolves around this singular body. Although other forces may be prominent in the charts of some individuals, still the

THE SUN

Sun is the total nucleus of being and symbolizes the complete potential of every human being alive. It is vitality and the life force. Your whole essence comes from the position of the Sun.

You are always trying to express the Sun according to its position by house and sign. Possibility for all development is found in the Sun, and it marks the fundamental character of your personal radiations all around you.

It symbolizes strength, vigor, ardor, generosity, and the ability to function effectively as a mature individual and a creative force in society. It is consciousness of the gift of life. The undeveloped solar nature is arrogant pushy, undependable, and proud, and is constantly using force.

MERCURY

Mercury is the planet closest to the Sun. It races around our star, gathering information and translating it to the rest of the system. Mercury represents your capacity to understand the desires of your own will and to translate those desires into action.

MERCURY

In other words it is the planet of mind and the power of communication. Through Mercury we develop an ability to think, write, speak, and observe—to become aware of the world around us. It colors our attitudes and vision of the world, as well as our capacity to communicate our inner responses to the outside world. Some people who have serious disabilities in their power of verbal communication have often wrongly been described as people lacking intelligence.

Although this planet (and its position in the horoscope) indicates your power to communicate your thoughts and perceptions to the world, intelligence is something deeper. Intelligence is distributed throughout all the planets. It is the relationship of the planets to each other that truly describes what we call intelligence. Mercury rules speaking, language, mathematics, draft and design, students, messengers, young people, offices, teachers, and any pursuits where the mind of man has wings.

VENUS

Venus is beauty. It symbolizes the harmony and radiance of a rare and elusive quality: beauty itself. It is refinement and delicacy, softness and charm. In astrology it indicates grace, balance, and the aesthetic sense. Where Venus is we see beauty, a gentle drawing in of energy and the need for satisfaction and completion. It is a special touch that finishes off rough edges.

VENUS

Venus is the planet of sensitivity and affection, and it is always the place for that other elusive phenomenon: love. Venus describes our sense of what is beautiful and loving. Poorly developed, it is vulgar, tasteless, and self-indulgent. But its ideal is the flame of spiritual love—Aphrodite, goddess of love, and the sweetness and power of personal beauty.

MARS

Mars is raw, crude energy. The planet next to Earth but outward from the Sun is a fiery red sphere that charges through the horoscope with force and fury. It represents the way you reach out for new adventure and new experience. It is energy drive, initiative, courage, daring. It is the power to start something and see it through. It can be thoughtless, cruel and wild, angry and hostile, causing cuts, burns, scalds, wounds. It can stab its way through a chart, or it can be the symbol of healthy spirited adventure, well-channeled constructive power to begin and keep up the drive.

MARS

If you have trouble starting things, if you lack the get-up-and-go to start the ball rolling, if you lack aggressiveness and self-confidence, chances are there's another planet influencing your Mars. Mars rules soldiers, butchers, surgeons, salespeople—in general any field that requires daring, bold skill, operational technique, or self-promotion.

JUPITER

Jupiter is the largest planet of the solar system. Planet Jupiter rules good luck and good cheer, health, wealth, optimism, happiness, success, joy. It is the symbol of opportunity and always opens the way for new possibilities in your life. It rules exuberance, enthusiasm, wisdom, knowledge, generosity, and all forms of expansion in general. It rules actors, statesmen, clerics, professional people, religion, publishing, and the distribution of many people over large areas.

JUPITER

Sometimes Jupiter makes you think you deserve everything, and you become sloppy, wasteful, careless and rude, prodigal and lawless, in the illusion that nothing can ever go wrong. Then there is the danger of your showing overconfidence, exaggeration, undependability, and overindulgence.

Jupiter is the minimization of limitation and the emphasis on spirituality and potential. It is the thirst for knowledge and higher learning.

SATURN

Saturn circles our system in dark splendor with its mysterious rings, forcing us to be awakened to whatever we have neglected in the past. It will present real puzzles and problems to be solved, causing delays, obstacles, and hindrances. By doing so, Saturn stirs our own sensitivity to those areas where we are laziest.

SATURN

Here we must patiently develop method, and only through painstaking effort can our ends be achieved. It brings order to a horoscope and imposes reason just where we are feeling least reasonable. By creating limitations and boundary, Saturn shows the consequences of being human and demands that we accept the changing cycles inevitable in human life. Saturn rules time, old age, and sobriety. It can bring depression, gloom, jealousy, and greed, or serious acceptance of responsibilities out of which success will develop. With Saturn there is nothing to do but face facts. It rules laborers, stones, granite, rocks, and crystals.

THE OUTER PLANETS: URANUS, NEPTUNE, PLUTO

Uranus, Neptune, and Pluto are the outer planets. They liberate human beings from cultural conditioning, and in that sense are the lawbreakers. In early times it was thought that Saturn was the last planet of the solar system—the outer limit beyond which we could never go. The discovery of the next three planets beyond Saturn ushered in new phases of human history, revolution, and technology.

URANUS

Uranus rules unexpected change, upheaval, revolution. It is the symbol of total independence and asserts the freedom of an individual from all restriction and restraint. It is a breakthrough planet and indicates talent, originality, and genius in a horoscope. It usually causes last-minute reversals and changes of plan, unwanted separations, accidents, catastrophes, and eccentric behavior. It can add irrational rebelliousness and perverse bohemianism to a personality or a streak of unaffected brilliance in science and art.

URANUS

Uranus rules technology, aviation, and all forms of electrical and electronic advancement. It governs great leaps forward and topsy-turvy situations, and always turns things around at the last minute. Its effects are difficult to predict, since it rules sudden last-minute decisions and events that come like lightning out of the blue.

NEPTUNE

Neptune dissolves existing reality the way the sea erodes the cliffs beside it. Its effects are subtle like the ringing of a buoy's bell in the fog. It suggests a reality higher than definition can usually describe. It awakens a sense of higher responsibility often causing guilt, worry, anxieties, or delusions. Neptune is associated with all forms of escape and can make things seem a certain way so convincingly that you are absolutely sure of something that eventually turns out to be quite different.

NEPTUNE

It is the planet of illusion and therefore governs the invisible realms that lie beyond our ordinary minds, beyond our simple factual ability to prove what is "real." Treachery, deceit, disillusionment, and disappointment are linked to Neptune. It describes a vague reality that promises eternity and the divine, yet in a manner so complex that we cannot really fathom it at all. At its worst Neptune is a cheap intoxicant; at its best it is the poetry, music, and inspiration of the higher planes of spiritual love. It has dominion over movies, photographs, and much of the arts.

PLUTO

Pluto lies at the outpost of our system and therefore rules finality in a horoscope—the final closing of chapters in your life, the passing of major milestones and points of development from which there is no return. It is a final wipeout, a closeout, an evacuation. It is a subtle but powerful catalyst in all transformations that occur. It creates, destroys, then recreates. Sometimes Pluto starts its influence with a minor event or insignificant incident that might even go unnoticed. Slowly but surely, little by little, everything changes, until at last there has been a total transformation in the area of your life where Pluto has been operating. It rules mass thinking and the trends that society first rejects, then adopts, and finally outgrows.

PLUTO

Pluto rules the dead and the underworld—all the powerful forces of creation and destruction that go on all the time beneath, around, and above us. It can bring a lust for power with strong obsessions.

It is the planet that rules the metamorphosis of the caterpillar into a butterfly, for it symbolizes the capacity to change totally and forever a person's lifestyle, way of thought, and behavior.

THE MOON

Exactly how does the Moon affect us psychologically and psychically? We know it controls the tides. We understand how it affects blood rhythm and body tides, together with all the chemical fluids that constitute our physical selves. Astronauts have walked upon its surface, and our scientists are now studying and analyzing data that will help determine the age of our satellite, its origin, and makeup.

THE MOON

But the true mystery of that small body as it circles our Earth each month remains hidden. Is it really a dead, lifeless body that has no light or heat of its own, reflecting only what the gigantic Sun throws toward it? Is it a sensitive reflecting device, which translates the blinding, billowing energy from our star into a language our bodies can understand?

In astrology, the Moon is said to rule our feelings, customs, habits, and moods. As the Sun is the constant, ever shining source of life in daytime, the Moon is our nighttime mother, lighting up the night and swiftly moving, reflecting ever so rapidly the changing phases of behavior and personality. If we feel happy or joyous, or we notice certain habits and repetitive feelings that bubble up from our dark centers then vanish as quickly as they appeared, very often it is the position of the Moon that describes these changes.

THE MOON IN ALL SIGNS

The Moon moves quickly through the Zodiac, that is, through all twelve signs of our Sun's apparent path. It stays in each sign for about 2¼ days. During its brief stay in a given sign, the moods and responses of people are always colored by the nature of that sign, any planets located there at that time, or any other heavenly bodies placed in such a way that the Moon will pick up their "vibration" as well. It's astonishing to observe how clearly the Moon changes people's interests and involvements as it moves along.

The following section gives brief descriptions of the Moon's influence in each sign.

MOON IN ARIES

There's excitement in the air. Some new little thing appears, and people are quick and full of energy and enterprise, ready for something new and turning on to a new experience. There's not much patience or hesitation, doubt or preoccupation with guilty self-damning recriminations. What's needed is action. People feel like putting their plans into operation. Pleasure and adventure characterize the mood, and it's time for things to change, pick up, improve. Confidence, optimism, positive feeling pervade the air. Sick people take a turn for the better. Life stirs with a feeling of renewal. People react bravely to challenges, with a sense of courage and dynamism. Self-reliance is the key word, and people minimize their problems and maximize the power to exercise freedom of the will. There is an air of abruptness and shortness of consideration, as people are feeling the courage of their convictions to do something for themselves. Feelings are strong and intuitive, and the mood is idealistic and freedom-oriented.

MOON IN TAURUS

Here the mood is just as pleasure loving, but less idealistic. Now the concerns are more materialistic, money-oriented, down-to-earth. The mood is stable, diligent, thoughtful, deliberate. It is a time when feelings are rich and deep, with a profound appreciation of the good things the world has to offer and the pleasures of the sensations. It is a period when people's minds are serious, realistic, and devoted to the increases and improvements of property and possessions and acquisition of wealth. There is a conservative tone, and people are fixed in their views, needing to add to their stability in every way. Assessment of assets, criticism, and the execution of tasks are strong involvements of the Taurus Moon when financial matters demand attention. It is devotion to security on a financial and emotional level. It is a fertile time, when ideas can begin to take root and grow.

MOON IN GEMINI

There is a rapid increase in movement. People are going places, exchanging ideas and information. Gossip and news travel fast under a Gemini Moon, because people are naturally involved with communication, finding out things from some, passing on information to others. Feelings shift to a mental level now, and people feel and say things that are sincere at the moment but lack the root and depth to endure much beyond the moment. People are involved with short-term engagements, quick trips. There is a definite need for changing the scene. You'll find people flirtatious and talkative, experimental and easygoing, falling into encounters they hadn't planned on. The mind is quick and active, with powers of writing and speaking greatly enhanced. Radio, television, letters, newspapers, magazines are in the spotlight with the Moon in Gemini, and new chances pop up for self-expression, with new people involved. Relatives and neighbors are tuned in to you and you to them. Take advantage of this fluidity of mind. It can rescue you from worldly involvements and get you into new surroundings for a short while.

MOON IN CANCER

Now you'll see people heading home. People turn their attention inward to their place of residence under a Cancer Moon. The active, changeable moods of yesterday vanish, and people settle in as if they were searching for a nest of security. Actually people are retiring, seeking to find peace and quiet within themselves. That's what they're feeling when they prefer to stay home rather than go out with a crowd of people to strange places. They need the warmth and comfort of the family and hearth. Maybe they feel anxious and insecure from the hustle and bustle of the workaday world. Maybe they're just tired. But it's definitely a time of tender need for emotional sustenance. It's a time for nostalgia and returning to times and places that once nourished deeply. Thoughts of parents, family, and old associations come to people. The heritage of their family ties holds them strongly now. These are personal needs that must be fed. Moods are deep and mysterious and sometimes sad. People are silent, psychic, and imaginative during this period. It's a fruitful time when people respond to love, food, and all the comforts of the inner world.

MOON IN LEO

The shift is back out in the world, and people are born again, like kids. They feel zestful, passionate, exuberant and need plenty of attention. They're interested in having a good time, enjoying themselves, and the world of entertainment takes over for a while. Places of amusement, theaters, parties, sprees, a whole gala of glamorous events, characterize this stage of the Moon's travel. Gracious, lavish hosting and a general feeling of buoyancy and flamboyance are in the air. It's a time of sunny, youthful fun when people are in the mood to take chances and win. The approach is direct, ardent, and strong. Bossy, authoritarian feelings predominate, and people throw themselves forward for all they're worth. Flattery is rampant, but the ego is vibrant and flourishing with the kiss of life, romance, and love. Speculation is indicated, and it's usually a time to go out and try your hand at love. Life is full and rich as a summer meadow, and feelings are warm.

MOON IN VIRGO

The party's over. Eyelashes are on the table. This is a time for cleaning up after the merrymakers have gone home. People are now concerned with sobering up and getting personal affairs straight, clearing up any confusions or undefined feelings from the night before, and generally attending to the practical business of doctoring up after the party. People are back at work, concerned with necessary, perhaps tedious tasks—paying bills, fixing and adjusting things, and generally purifying their lives, streamlining their affairs, and involving themselves with work and service to the community. Purity is the key word in personal habits, diet, and emotional needs. Propriety and coolness take the place of yesterday's devil-may-care passion, and the results are a detached, inhibited period under a Virgo

Moon. Feelings are not omitted; they are merely subjected to the scrutiny of the mind and thus purified. Health comes to the fore, and people are interested in clearing up problems.

MOON IN LIBRA

Here there is a mood of harmony, when people strive to join with other people in a bond of peace and justice. At this time people need relationships and often seek the company of others in a smooth-flowing feeling of love, beauty, and togetherness. People make efforts to understand other people, and though it's not the best time to make decisions, many situations keep presenting themselves from the outside to change plans and offer new opportunities. There is a general search for accord between partners, and differences are explored as similarities are shared. The tone is concilatory, and the mood is one of cooperation, patience, and tolerance. People do not generally feel independent, and sometimes this need to share or lean on others disturbs them. It shouldn't. This is the moment for uniting and sharing, for feeling a mutual flow of kindness and tenderness between people. The air is ingratiating and sometimes lacks stamina, courage, and a consistent, definite point of view. But it is a time favoring the condition of beauty and the development of all forms of art.

MOON IN SCORPIO

This is not a mood of sharing. It's driving, intense, brooding—full of passion and desire. Its baser aspects are the impulses of selfishness, cruelty, and the pursuit of animal drives and appetites. There is a craving for excitement and a desire to battle and win in a blood-thirsty war for survival. It is competitive and ruthless, sarcastic and easily bruised, highly sexual and touchy, without being especially tender. Retaliation, jealousy, and revenge can be felt too during this time. Financial involvements, debts, and property issues arise now. Powerful underworld forces are at work here, and great care is needed to transform ignorance into wisdom, to keep the mind from descending into the lower depths. During the Moon's stay in Scorpio we contact the dark undercurrents swirling around and get in touch with a magical part of our natures. Interest lies in death, inheritance, and the powers of rebirth and regeneration.

MOON IN SAGITTARIUS

Here the mind climbs out of the depths, and people are involved with the higher, more enlightened, and conscious facets of their personality. There's a renewed interest in learning, education, and philosophy, and a new involvement with ethics, morals, national and international issues: a concern with looking for a better way to live. It's a time of general improvement, with people feeling more deeply hopeful and optimistic. They are dreaming of new places, new possibilities, new horizons. They are emerging from the abyss and leaving the past behind, with their eyes gazing toward the new horizon. They decide to travel, or renew their contacts with those far away. They question their religious beliefs and investigate new areas of metaphysical inquiry. It's a time for adventure, sports, playing the field—people have their eye on new possibilities. They are bored with depression and details. They feel restless and optimistic, joyous and delighted to be alive. Thoughts revolve around adventure, travel, liberation.

MOON IN CAPRICORN

When the Moon moves into Capricorn, things slow down considerably. People require a quiet, organized, and regularized condition. Their minds are sober and realistic, and they are methodically going about bringing their dreams and plans into reality. They are more conscious of what is standing between them and success, and during this time they take definite, decisive steps to remove any obstacles from their path. They are cautious, suspicious, sometimes depressed, discouraged, and gloomy, but they are more determined than ever to accomplish their tasks. They take care of responsibilities now, wake up to facts, and wrestle with problems and dilemmas of this world. They are politically minded and concerned with social convention now, and it is under a Capricorn Moon that conditioning and conformity elicit the greatest responses. People are moderate and serious and surround themselves with what is most familiar. They want predictable situations and need time to think deeply and deliberately about all issues. It's a time for planning.

MOON IN AQUARIUS

Spontaneity replaces the sober predictability of yesterday. Now events, people, and situations pop up, and you take advantage of unsought opportunities and can expect the unexpected. Surprises, reversals, and shifts in plans mark this period. There is a resurgence of optimism, and things you wouldn't expect to happen suddenly do. What you were absolutely sure was going to happen simply doesn't. Here there is a need for adventure born from a healthy curiosity that characterizes people's moods. Unrealistic utopias are dreamed of, and it is from such idealistic dreams that worlds of the future are built. There is a renewed interest in friendship, comradeship, community, and union on high planes of mental and spiritual companionship. People free each other from grudges or long-standing deadlocks, and there is a hopeful joining of hands in a spirit of love and peace. People don't feel like sticking to previous plans, and they must be able to respond to new situations at the last minute. People need freedom. Groups of people come together and meet, perhaps for a common purpose of having dinner or hearing music, and leave knowing each other better.

MOON IN PISCES

Flashes of brilliant insight and mysterious knowledge characterize the Moon's passage in Pisces. Sometimes valuable "truths" seem to emerge which, later in the light of day, turn out to be false. This is a time of poetry, intuition, and music, when worldly realities can be the most illusory and unreliable of all. There are often feelings of remorse, guilt, or sorrow connected with a Pisces Moon—sorrow from the childhood or family or past. Confusion, anxiety, worry, and a host of imagined pains and sorrows may drag you down until you cannot move or think. Often there are connections with hospitals, prisons, alcohol, drugs, and lower forms of escape. It is a highly emotional time, when the feelings and compassion for humanity and all people everywhere rise to the surface of your being. Mysteries of society and the soul now rise to demand solutions, but often the riddles posed during this period have many answers that all seem right. It is more a time for inner reflection than positive action. It is a time when poetry and music float to the surface of the being, and for the creative artist it is the richest source of inspiration.

MOON TABLES

CORRECTION FOR NEW YORK TIME, FIVE HOURS WEST OF GREENWICH

Atlanta, Boston, Detroit, Miami, Washington, Montreal, Ottawa, Quebec, Bogota, Havana, Lima, Santiago.......................Same time

Chicago, New Orleans, Houston, Winnipeg, Churchill, Mexico City...............................Deduct 1 hour

Albuquerque, Denver, Phoenix, El Paso, Edmonton, Helena....................................Deduct 2 hours

Los Angeles, San Francisco, Reno, Portland, Seattle, Vancouver.......................Deduct 3 hours

Honolulu, Anchorage, Fairbanks, Kodiak...Deduct 5 hours

Nome, Samoa, Tonga, Midway.............Deduct 6 hours

Halifax, Bermuda, San Juan, Caracas, La Paz, Barbados.....................................Add 1 hour

St. John's, Brasilia, Rio de Janeiro, Sao Paulo, Buenos Aires, Montevideo..................Add 2 hours

Azores, Cape Verde Islands....................Add 3 hours

Canary Islands, Madeira, Reykjavik...........Add 4 hours

London, Paris, Amsterdam, Madrid, Lisbon, Gibraltar, Belfast, Rabat.....................Add 5 hours

Frankfurt, Rome, Oslo, Stockholm, Prague, Belgrade.......................................Add 6 hours

Bucharest, Beirut, Tel Aviv, Athens, Istanbul, Cairo, Alexandria, Cape Town, Johannesburg......Add 7 hours

Moscow, Leningrad, Baghdad, Dhahran, Addis Ababa, Nairobi, Teheran, Zanzibar...Add 8 hours

Bombay, Calcutta, Sri Lanka...............Add 10 ½ hours

Hong Kong, Shanghai, Manila, Peking, Perth.......................................Add 13 hours

Tokyo, Okinawa, Darwin, Pusan.............Add 14 hours

Sydney, Melbourne, Port Moresby, Guam....Add 15 hours

Auckland, Wellington, Suva, Wake...........Add 17 hours

2003 MOON SIGN DATES—NEW YORK TIME

JANUARY Day Moon Enters		FEBRUARY Day Moon Enters		MARCH Day Moon Enters	
1. Capric.	6:44 pm	1. Aquar.		1. Pisces	10:27 pm
2. Capric.		2. Pisces	2:56 pm	2. Pisces	
3. Aquar.	10:58 pm	3. Pisces		3. Pisces	
4. Aquar.		4. Pisces		4. Aries	8:31 am
5. Aquar.		5. Aries	12:45 am	5. Aries	
6. Pisces	5:58 am	6. Aries		6. Taurus	8:37 pm
7. Pisces		7. Taurus	1:00 pm	7. Taurus	
8. Aries	4:16 pm	8. Taurus		8. Taurus	
9. Aries		9. Taurus		9. Gemini	9:39 am
10. Aries		10. Gemini	1:46 am	10. Gemini	
11. Taurus	4:49 am	11. Gemini		11. Cancer	9:13 pm
12. Taurus		12. Cancer	12:20 pm	12. Cancer	
13. Gemini	5:09 pm	13. Cancer		13. Cancer	
14. Gemini		14. Leo	7:05 pm	14. Leo	5:07 am
15. Gemini		15. Leo		15. Leo	
16. Cancer	2:57 am	16. Virgo	10:24 pm	16. Virgo	8:54 am
17. Cancer		17. Virgo		17. Virgo	
18. Leo	9:30 am	18. Libra	11:49 pm	18. Libra	9:44 am
19. Leo		19. Libra		19. Libra	
20. Virgo	1:33 pm	20. Libra		20. Scorp.	9:39 am
21. Virgo		21. Scorp.	1:10 am	21. Scorp.	
22. Libra	4:24 pm	22. Scorp.		22. Sagitt.	10:34 am
23. Libra		23. Sagitt.	3:47 am	23. Sagitt.	
24. Scorp.	7:10 pm	24. Sagitt.		24. Capric.	1:49 pm
25. Scorp.		25. Capric.	8:12 am	25. Capric.	
26. Sagitt.	10:27 pm	26. Capric.		26. Aquar.	7:52 pm
27. Sagitt.		27. Aquar.	2:26 pm	27. Aquar.	
28. Sagitt.		28. Aquar.		28. Aquar.	
29. Capric.	2:31 am			29. Pisces	4:27 am
30. Capric.				30. Pisces	
31. Aquar.	7:45 am			31. Aries	3:06 pm

Summer time to be considered where applicable.

2003 MOON SIGN DATES—NEW YORK TIME

APRIL		MAY		JUNE	
Day Moon Enters		**Day Moon Enters**		**Day Moon Enters**	
1. Aries		1. Taurus		1. Cancer	4:28 pm
2. Aries		2. Gemini	10:28 pm	2. Cancer	
3. Taurus	3:21 am	3. Gemini		3. Cancer	
4. Taurus		4. Gemini		4. Leo	2:26 am
5. Gemini	4:25 pm	5. Cancer	10:43 am	5. Leo	
6. Gemini		6. Cancer		6. Virgo	9:52 am
7. Gemini		7. Leo	8:47 pm	7. Virgo	
8. Cancer	4:37 am	8. Leo		8. Libra	2:31 pm
9. Cancer		9. Leo		9. Libra	
10. Leo	1:55 pm	10. Virgo	3:32 am	10. Scorp.	4:40 pm
11. Leo		11. Virgo		11. Scorp.	
12. Virgo	7:08 pm	12. Libra	6:43 am	12. Sagitt.	5:13 pm
13. Virgo		13. Libra		13. Sagitt.	
14. Libra	8:43 pm	14. Scorp.	7:15 am	14. Capric.	5:39 pm
15. Libra		15. Scorp.		15. Capric.	
16. Scorp.	8:17 pm	16. Sagitt.	6:44 am	16. Aquar.	7:42 pm
17. Scorp.		17. Sagitt.		17. Aquar.	
18. Sagitt.	7:53 pm	18. Capric.	7:04 am	18. Aquar.	
19. Sagitt.		19. Capric.		19. Pisces	12:58 am
20. Capric.	9:21 pm	20. Aquar.	10:02 am	20. Pisces	
21. Capric.		21. Aquar.		21. Aries	10:07 am
22. Capric.		22. Pisces	4:42 pm	22. Aries	
23. Aquar.	1:59 am	23. Pisces		23. Taurus	10:16 pm
24. Aquar.		24. Pisces		24. Taurus	
25. Pisces	10:03 am	25. Aries	3:00 am	25. Taurus	
26. Pisces		26. Aries		26. Gemini	11:14 am
27. Aries	8:55 pm	27. Taurus	3:33 am	27. Gemini	
28. Aries		28. Taurus		28. Cancer	10:53 pm
29. Aries		29. Taurus		29. Cancer	
30. Taurus	9:27 am	30. Gemini	4:33 am	30. Cancer	
		31. Gemini			

Summer time to be considered where applicable.

2003 MOON SIGN DATES—NEW YORK TIME

JULY		AUGUST		SEPTEMBER	
Day Moon Enters		**Day Moon Enters**		**Day Moon Enters**	
1. Leo	8:14 am	1. Virgo		1. Scorp.	
2. Leo		2. Libra	1:49 am	2. Sagitt.	1:33 pm
3. Virgo	3:17 pm	3. Libra		3. Sagitt.	
4. Virgo		4. Scorp.	5:13 am	4. Capric.	4:52 pm
5. Libra	8:21 pm	5. Scorp.		5. Capric.	
6. Libra		6. Sagitt.	8:12 am	6. Aquar.	9:16 pm
7. Scorp.	11:45 pm	7. Sagitt.		7. Aquar.	
8. Scorp.		8. Capric.	11:03 am	8. Aquar.	
9. Scorp.		9. Capric.		9. Pisces	3:08 am
10. Sagitt.	1:49 am	10. Aquar.	2:25 pm	10. Pisces	
11. Sagitt.		11. Aquar.		11. Aries	11:10 am
12. Capric.	3:22 am	12. Pisces	7:20 pm	12. Aries	
13. Capric.		13. Pisces		13. Taurus	9:51 pm
14. Aquar.	5:39 am	14. Pisces		14. Taurus	
15. Aquar.		15. Aries	3:01 am	15. Taurus	
16. Pisces	10:15 am	16. Aries		16. Gemini	10:33 am
17. Pisces		17. Taurus	1:53 pm	17. Gemini	
18. Aries	6:21 pm	18. Taurus		18. Cancer	11:08 pm
19. Aries		19. Taurus		19. Cancer	
20. Aries		20. Gemini	2:42 am	20. Cancer	
21. Taurus	5:49 am	21. Gemini		21. Leo	9:04 am
22. Taurus		22. Cancer	2:45 pm	22. Leo	
23. Gemini	6:43 pm	23. Cancer		23. Virgo	3:06 pm
24. Gemini		24. Leo	11:49 pm	24. Virgo	
25. Gemini		25. Leo		25. Libra	5:50 pm
26. Cancer	6:24 am	26. Leo		26. Libra	
27. Cancer		27. Virgo	5:28 am	27. Scorp.	6:53 pm
28. Leo	3:18 pm	28. Virgo		28. Scorp.	
29. Leo		29. Libra	8:42 am	29. Sagitt.	7:58 pm
30. Virgo	9:28 pm	30. Libra		30. Sagitt.	
31. Virgo		31. Scorp.	11:01 am		

Summer time to be considered where applicable.

2003 MOON SIGN DATES—NEW YORK TIME

OCTOBER		
Day	**Moon Enters**	
1.	Capric.	10:22 pm
2.	Capric.	
3.	Capric.	
4.	Aquar.	2:46 am
5.	Aquar.	
6.	Pisces	9:21 am
7.	Pisces	
8.	Aries	6:09 pm
9.	Aries	
10.	Aries	
11.	Taurus	5:06 am
12.	Taurus	
13.	Gemini	5:46 pm
14.	Gemini	
15.	Gemini	
16.	Cancer	6:42 am
17.	Cancer	
18.	Leo	5:42 pm
19.	Leo	
20.	Leo	
21.	Virgo	1:02 am
22.	Virgo	
23.	Libra	4:28 am
24.	Libra	
25.	Scorp.	5:10 am
26.	Scorp.	
27.	Sagitt.	4:56 am
28.	Sagitt.	
29.	Capric.	5:38 am
30.	Capric.	
31.	Aquar.	8:42 am

NOVEMBER		
Day	**Moon Enters**	
1.	Aquar.	
2.	Pisces	2:53 am
3.	Pisces	
4.	Pisces	
5.	Aries	12:04 am
6.	Aries	
7.	Taurus	11:30 am
8.	Taurus	
9.	Taurus	
10.	Gemini	12:15 am
11.	Gemini	
12.	Cancer	1:11 pm
13.	Cancer	
14.	Cancer	
15.	Leo	12:49 am
16.	Leo	
17.	Virgo	9:37 am
18.	Virgo	
19.	Libra	2:43 pm
20.	Libra	
21.	Scorp.	4:25 pm
22.	Scorp.	
23.	Sagitt.	4:04 pm
24.	Sagitt.	
25.	Capric.	3:32 pm
26.	Capric.	
27.	Aquar.	4:49 pm
28.	Aquar.	
29.	Pisces	9:26 pm
30.	Pisces	

DECEMBER		
Day	**Moon Enters**	
1.	Pisces	
2.	Aries	5:57 am
3.	Aries	
4.	Taurus	5:31 pm
5.	Taurus	
6.	Taurus	
7.	Gemini	6:27 am
8.	Gemini	
9.	Cancer	7:12 pm
10.	Cancer	
11.	Cancer	
12.	Leo	6:41 am
13.	Leo	
14.	Virgo	4:08 pm
15.	Virgo	
16.	Libra	10:48 pm
17.	Libra	
18.	Libra	
19.	Scorp.	2:21 am
20.	Scorp.	
21.	Sagitt.	3:17 am
22.	Sagitt.	
23.	Capric.	2:56 am
24.	Capric.	
25.	Aquar.	3:14 am
26.	Aquar.	
27.	Pisces	6:11 am
28.	Pisces	
29.	Aries	1:09 pm
30.	Aries	
31.	Aries	

Summer time to be considered where applicable.

2003 FISHING GUIDE

	Good	Best
January	10-15-18-19-20-21	2-16-17-25
February	1-15-16-17-18-23	9-13-14-19
March	11-15-16-17-18	3-19-20-21-25
April	1-13-14-19-23	9-15-16-17-18
May	1-9-16-17-18-31	13-14-15-19-23
June	7-13-14-17-21	11-12-15-16-29
July	10-11-14-15-16-21-29	7-12-13
August	10-11-12-15-20-27	5-9-13-14
September	3-7-8-11-12-13-18	9-10-26
October	9-10-11	2-7-8-12-13-18-25
November	1-6-7-10-11-12-17-23	8-9-30
December	7-8-9-16-30	5-6-10-11-23

2003 PLANTING GUIDE

	Aboveground Crops	Root Crops
January	3-7-11-12-13-16-17	23-24-25-26-29-30
February	3-4-8-9-13-14	19-20-21-22-26
March	3-7-8-12-13	2-19-20-21-25-26-29-30
April	3-4-8-9-15	17-18-21-22-26-27
May	2-6-7-13-14-15	19-23-24-28-29
June	2-3-9-10-11-12-30	15-16-19-20-24-25
July	6-7-8-9-12	17-18-22-23-27
August	2-3-4-5-9-30-31	13-14-18-19-23-24
September	1-5-6-9-26-27-28-29	14-15-19-20
October	2-3-7-8-26-30	12-13-17-18-23-24
November	3-4-8-26-30	9-13-14-20-21-22
December	1-5-6-23-24-28	10-11-17-18-19-20

	Pruning	Weeds and Pests
January	25-26	1-19-20-21-27-28
February	21-22	17-18-23-24-28
March	2-21-29-30	1-23-27-28
April	17-18-26-27	19-20-23-24-28-29
May	23-24	17-21-25-26-30
June	19-20	17-18-22-23-27-28
July	17-18-27	15-19-20-24-25
August	13-14-23-24	12-15-16-20-21-25-26
September	19-20	12-13-17-18-22-23-24-25
October	17-18	10-14-15-19-20-21-22
November	13-14-22	10-11-15-16-17-18
December	10-11-19-20	9-13-14-15-16-21-22

2003 PHASES OF THE MOON—NEW YORK TIME

New Moon	First Quarter	Full Moon	Last Quarter
Jan. 2	Jan. 10	Jan. 18	Jan. 25
Feb. 1	Feb. 9	Feb. 16	Feb. 23
March 2	March 11	March 18	March 24
April 1	April 9	April 16	April 23
May 1	May 9	May 15	May 22
May 30	June 7	June 14	June 21
June 29	July 6	July 13	July 21
July 29	Aug. 5	Aug. 11	Aug. 19
Aug. 27	Sept. 3	Sept. 10	Sept. 18
Sept. 25	Oct. 2	Oct. 10	Oct. 18
Oct. 25	Oct. 31	Nov. 8	Nov. 16
Nov. 23	Nov. 30	Dec. 8	Dec. 16
Dec. 23	Dec. 30	Jan. 7 ('04)	Jan. 15 ('04)

Each phase of the Moon lasts approximately seven to eight days, during which the Moon's shape gradually changes as it comes out of one phase and goes into the next.

There will be a solar eclipse during the New Moon phase on May 30 and November 23.

There will be a lunar eclipse during the Full Moon phase on May 15 and November 8.

Use the Moon phases to connect you with your lucky numbers for this year. See the next page (page 112) and your lucky numbers.

LUCKY NUMBERS
FOR LEO: 2003

Lucky numbers and astrology can be linked through the movements of the Moon. Each phase of the thirteen Moon cycles vibrates with a sequence of numbers for your Sign of the Zodiac over the course of the year. Using your lucky numbers is a fun system that connects you with tradition.

New Moon	First Quarter	Full Moon	Last Quarter
Jan. 2	Jan. 10	Jan. 18	Jan. 25
1 0 6 8	8 3 7 4	4 0 7 1	0 8 6 5
Feb. 1	Feb. 9	Feb. 16	Feb. 23
0 2 4 8	8 3 9 6	6 7 4 2	9 8 7 5
March 2	March 11	March 18	March 24
7 7 2 6	6 3 9 1	4 2 4 2	2 1 0 7
April 1	April 9	April 16	April 23
7 9 4 8	5 2 3 6	6 4 2 7	6 4 6 0
May 1	May 9	May 15	May 22
4 5 2 8	8 9 3 0	0 8 7 6	5 3 5 9
May 30	June 7	June 14	June 21
8 0 7 8	8 2 9 7	7 6 5 3	5 2 6 0
June 29	July 6	July 13	July 21
5 4 5 8	8 6 4 3	3 2 9 2	2 6 9 6
July 29	August 5	August 11	August 19
6 2 4 7	5 3 2 0	1 8 0 5	5 9 1 7
August 27	Sept. 3	Sept. 10	Sept. 18
7 3 2 9	7 6 5 3	3 5 9 4	4 1 7 9
Sept. 25	Oct. 2	Oct. 10	Oct. 18
6 0 8 7	7 9 4 6	6 1 5 2	2 8 9 6
Oct. 25	Oct. 31	Nov. 8	Nov. 16
6 4 2 1	9 7 9 4	4 8 5 2	2 3 6 7
Nov. 23	Nov. 30	Dec. 8	Dec. 16
2 4 0 3	1 0 3 7	2 8 5 6	6 9 7 0
Dec. 23	Dec. 30	Jan. 7 ('04)	Jan. 15 ('04)
1 0 8 6	8 8 3 7	5 5 3 1	9 1 8 6

LEO
YEARLY FORECAST: 2003

*Forecast for 2003 Concerning Business
Prospects, Financial Affairs, Health,
Travel, Employment, Love and Marriage
for Persons Born with the Sun
in the Zodiacal Sign of Leo,
July 21–August 21.*

This year promises to be a reflective and enlivening one for those of you born under the influence of the Sun in the zodiacal sign of Leo, whose ruler is the warm and brilliant Sun. The urge to develop your talents will be quite strong, and you may take up new interests as well. Your sense of optimism will be higher than usual, bringing within range more chances to make positive changes to your life. In the business world, it looks as if a position of greater power would suit you. Your enterprise may also benefit from branching out into more creative areas of production. The outlook for personal finances suggests a year when there may be opportunities to make unusual investments. But you will almost certainly have to watch your spending, which could get a bit excessive at times. Your health should remain good, especially if you can learn to listen more closely to your body's needs. Try to avoid indulging too much in rich foods, no matter how strong the temptation. Travel prospects focus upon the likelihood of a romantic encounter, but it may turn out to be more profound than expected. Coming into contact with different cultures can be a life-changing experience. Where jobs are concerned, there is quite a lot of emphasis on developing your current role rather than changing direction. However, those of you who are looking around might think about teaching. The world of love and romance has lessons to teach about give and take, so that your partner's needs are met as well as your own. A deeper sense of trust can be achieved if you are able to allow your beloved more freedom within the relationship, and this should prove to be one of the most firm foundations for your happiness both now and in the future.

The year 2003 seems to be a promising period for consolidating a position of power in the business world. If you've been on the sidelines up until now, you will probably find yourself quite naturally coming forward into the limelight. It's necessary to be sure you can live up to increased responsibilities on all levels of the enterprise. This is a year during which rival companies may begin to play dirty, using underhand or even illegal methods to win a share of your market. While it will be vital to fight back, you should under no circumstances risk your reputation in any way. Whatever your business, it seems there are profits to be made by finding ways to tap into the inherent romantic nature of humankind. Perhaps a carefully planned advertising campaign would give your company a higher profile, by appealing to the basic human need to love and be loved; but of course this has to be done tastefully. A spot of lateral thinking may be in order to liven up the image of your company if it appears outmoded or stuffy in any way. Rather than going along tried and tested lines, experiment a bit with creative ideas and see if they turn out to be effective. If you are in a business partnership, be prepared for a few disagreements over the course of the year. What is going to be essential is that you are able to work out all important decisions in tandem, rather than one or both of you attempting to act independently. During the period between March and September your finances may come under the beady eye of officialdom. It may be wise to spend the first couple of months of the year making sure that everything is in apple-pie order. The spring period may bring minor troubles with employees; if so, you should approach any disagreements with as open a mind as possible. From June onward is a promising time to start researching the possibility of servicing new or unexplored markets which have been overlooked by other companies. Results may be slow in coming, but should prove quite lucrative as time passes. Your best route to success this year seems to lie in giving positive and enthusiastic leadership, which can inspire colleagues and employees to pull together toward ambitious goals.

Your personal finances may suffer a little if you insist on keeping up a luxurious lifestyle which is not realistic, given your budget. In fact, it will be very unwise to allow a fantasy lifestyle to overtake your sense of what's practical. So throttle back a bit if resources seem to be getting low. This is a period when you seem well able to take on a second job if necessary, since your energy and willingness to work seem higher than usual. Romance can prove a bit of a drain on your money, especially if you're set on trying to impress a new partner with expensive treats as well as by looking your absolute best. Try to remember that he or she actually is more interested in your personality than in what you can provide; love that can be bought isn't worth having anyway. During the spring and summer there may be opportunities to make sound investments, which would help secure your future. However, take expert advice if you are thinking of sinking funds into anything risky. As long as you can get used to juggling money around a bit, this year will be financially quite positive.

Your health ought to remain fairly good just as long as you are willing to be sensible and not excessive in your behavior. In fact, you will probably be feeling quite buoyant as the year begins; but that shouldn't be taken as a sign that you can get away with anything. Instead, try to build on this feeling of well-being by making extra efforts to keep fit. You may develop a tendency to put on weight as the year passes, which can be quite unexpected. The answer here is simply to watch what you eat and to make sure you get some exercise every day; walking can be excellent, especially if you habitually drive everywhere. Try not to brood on stresses and problems, as that can drain your energy. Adopting a practical approach will on the other hand energize you, by making you feel more in control of life. Busy periods should be followed by a couple of days of proper relaxation. Make sure you are getting enough sleep too. Enjoying life without a sense of urgency or rush can be the best recipe for well-being.

Your enthusiasm for travel this year may have a specific reason: that of a yearning for a holiday romance. In fact, this is in the cards; but it is likely to be a deeper and even more disturbing experience than you expect. Use a bit of caution before getting involved with anyone who could present problems later on. Business trips ought to be quite productive, although you will tend to find them tiring. This may be partly due to the need to get along with colleagues while traveling, but making the effort to develop a more friendly relationship will be well worthwhile. Inner travel seems as important as actual globe-trotting at the moment. Exploring new horizons of thought can be as stimulating as finding a new beach, but it's also true that visiting unknown places can act as a stimulus to your imagination. Vacations taken after August may prove more expensive than anticipated, but they can also furnish you with vivid and pleasurable memories.

The outlook for jobs and employment appears reasonably stable, which is good news if you are happy in your current position. The emphasis seems to be on developing skills which will enable you to diversify more, and perhaps earn a higher salary. You have many personal talents and traits which can enrich your work, and these should be allowed to shine out in some field or other. Those of you who are in fact looking around for a change of direction may begin to think about teaching as a career. It needn't be either time-consuming or expensive to train, and the work can be deeply satisfying, as well as giving you a chance to put on a show. The possibility of launching your own business may appear quite attractive, especially in partnership with a friend. However, take a bit of time to research this, as it could turn out to be much more of a full-time commitment than anticipated. Working for a charity can be an excellent way to bring your ideals into play in the field of work. It should also make you feel pretty positive about yourself, since you will be making a useful contribution toward the good of the world. You Leos tend to be big-hearted and generous, and it would be wonderful to use these traits in your job.

Where love and romance are concerned, it looks as if there are some very positive experiences awaiting you. But remember that this isn't just about having a good time, but about learning how other people work and what you can do to make them happy. No relationship is without its share of problems, and it would be foolish to think otherwise. Learning to sort them out rather than running at the first sign of trouble can mark a big step in your personal development. If you have been single for a while, be prepared to be swept off your feet by someone who tears up the relationship rule book. It will almost certainly do you good to be made to think differently, but do your best to maintain a sense of independence as well. Those of you in a settled partnership are bound to go through a couple of lows as well as high points. There is a possibility of spending some time apart from your beloved, which may help you both get a better sense of perspective. The secret of true love lies in your wanting to make your partner happy; and learning to do so even at the expense of your own comfort can lead to deeper and more enriching relationships.

LEO
DAILY FORECAST: 2003

1st Week/January 1–7

Wednesday January 1st. You want to be active to start the year. Outdoor activities can help you to feel refreshed if you had a late night. Try cross-country skiing, or go for a tramp in the woods. A long and trusted friend may do something that upsets you. The intentions are likely to be honorable, even if it may not look that way. Ask what the story is.

Thursday the 2nd. Whatever project you start now can bear fruit within the coming month. This can be an especially good time to think about career goals, and to implement strategies to achieve them. You may be thinking about changing your diet at this time. Some of you may be turning vegetarian. You should have the discipline to do so now.

Friday the 3rd. An unexpected romantic attraction can take you by surprise. You may bump into this person at the health food store or close to your place of business. Take things slowly, even if you feel like jumping in feet first. New and innovative methods may be worth considering in connection with your work now. You can be seen as someone ahead of the times.

Saturday the 4th. Wires may get crossed when communicating with others. Double-check all appointment times before leaving. Be sure to allow extra travel time, probably due to traffic tie-ups right now. Expect dates to be late, if they show up at all. Your best bet is to stay flexible. Avoid making any irrevocable decisions at this time.

Sunday the 5th. Your primary relationship is likely to be a major part of the day's scenario. You can be friends now as well as romantic partners. Do something active and fun together this afternoon. Get involved in a humanitarian cause or charity drive together. Be careful with your words now, however, as others could take your blunt honesty the wrong way.

Monday the 6th. This is a good time to check on your investments, retirement accounts, and insurance policies. See what needs renewing and what needs reviewing. You can see the bigger picture now, and may feel impatient about achieving your goals. Avoid biting off more than you can chew. Be moderate and consistent to come out ahead.

Tuesday the 7th. A vague sense of irritation may permeate the day. Figure out what it is that is really bothering you, and take some assertive steps to solve things. You should feel powerful and energized as a result. Leave the details of a money management deal to the experts. You may not know enough to take care of it on your own.

Weekly Summary

Pay attention to your mental and physical state this week. Any health upsets may be caused by tensions you have encountered at work or at home. Take time out to pamper yourself and to relax. Work out a strategy on how best to handle the situation, and then take some practical steps toward that goal. Your physical body is likely to respond positively as a result.

You can be considering an alliance of some sort at this time. A mutually formed partnership arrangement will work out well as long as you both are clear on how best to attain your mutual goals. You each have your own area of expertise, and together you will make an unbeatable team.

It may be time to start dealing with any debt you accrued over the last few months. Nipping it in the bud this week can prevent any undue interest from mounting up. It is likely to be credit cards that are causing all the trouble. Resolve to use cash whenever possible from now on. You should have the discipline to do what is best for your financial future.

2nd Week/January 8–14

Wednesday the 8th. You seem to sense how other people are really feeling. You can use this skill when negotiating in business or when talking to a dear friend. You can be subtly assertive and should be able to handle confrontation in a way that allows for a win-win situation. Take a swim, a hot tub, or a bath to relax this evening.

Thursday the 9th. You probably are in an optimistic and energetic frame of mind. The sky may be the limit now where you are concerned, and you should be able to take practical steps forward in any travel or educational plans. A colleague or authority figure may burden you by asking for supporting data for a project now, so be ready with the facts.

Friday the 10th. A decision you made a week ago can be up for review. Make the necessary adjustments, and see what happens. It may still be a very viable idea. You may abhor details now because they tend to slow you down. Delegate them to more pragmatic colleagues, or put them on hold for another time when you have more patience.

Saturday the 11th. You probably are feeling quite restless. You may be more inclined than usual to take risks now as a result. Just be sure that they are calculated ones. Money matters may need some attention this afternoon. Set up a budget that you can stick to, allowing for the occasional luxury or indulgence. Being too stringent can only backfire.

Sunday the 12th. Family matters can be part of the scenario at present. Attend an extended family gathering this afternoon, or host one yourself. Good food can put everyone into a happy and contented mood. Guard against developing a stubborn attitude with an older man. Try to see his point of view, as there may be some wisdom in it.

Monday the 13th. Hard work is fulfilling just now, and you should get much accomplished. You may find yourself interacting with bigwigs this afternoon, so dress and grooming are important. You seem to be sensible in your attitude, and you may stick with work methods that are tried and true. A child may require some extra affection and attention this evening.

Tuesday the 14th. You can expect to be on the go, busily running errands and returning phone calls. You may be involved in group activities, surrounded by people whom you do not know very well. Some of these people can become very good friends, especially if you join a cause or a humanitarian effort that has meaning for you.

Weekly Summary

Check out vacation plans while you have time and are in the mood. Work is likely to be slow for the next little while, so take advantage of it. You may not get another period like it for a while. A partner may want to get in on the action and help to plan your itinerary. Try to combine rest and relaxation with some fun and adventure too.

It may be prudent to avoid mixing business with pleasure at this time. A romantic attraction can be mutual between you and someone at work. Consider the consequences if it doesn't work out. Decide whether you would be able to continue to work with the person in a congenial way. You may be happier as friends anyway.

Expand your social circle by getting involved in a community activity. Pick a political candidate whom you admire and help him or her to campaign. Volunteer to help a local humanitarian effort. Your presence can add to the profile of the endeavor, and you may be asked to take charge of a specific action group.

3rd Week/January 15–21

Wednesday the 15th. Adventures of the mind can be stimulating as well as illuminating. You may find yourself involved in a discussion group of some sort. Expect to come up with some brilliant ideas as you bounce ideas off other people. A close friend may ask a very important favor of you this evening. Grant it only if it feels right.

Thursday the 16th. Your intuition may be working overtime, or you can be just plain lucky. Things can work out well for you now as long as you do what you feel is right. Carrying out domestic duties can bring pleasure at this time. Spend time sprucing up your living area. Add things that make you feel secure and cozy.

Friday the 17th. You can feel an increased need for privacy. Try to work from home if you can get more quiet time there. This appears to be a good day to make plans and strategies to implement in the future. Avoid the spotlight. Rest and solitude can help you to recharge and revitalize. Rent a good movie this evening.

Saturday the 18th. This promises to be a memorable day for you as the Moon enters your sign. Information may come to light that enables you to make a final decision about a relationship or about an issue within a relationship. Interactions with others may be intense at this time, but this should enable you to get to the core of the matter and deal with it.

Sunday the 19th. You may find yourself instinctively taking charge of a recreational outing. Others will naturally look to you for leadership now, and you can take this position on with ease. You may come across as larger than life, but your humor should win over even the stodgiest of people. This can be a good time for creative types to put their work on display.

Monday the 20th. Money matters can be taking up much of your time at present. A financial deal hatched now will work out to your benefit in the long run. Working in tandem with a partner may increase your odds of success. As you may be dealing with buying or selling property or possessions at this time, read the fine print before signing anything.

Tuesday the 21st. Your big heart can reach out to envelop everybody with whom you come in contact. Your generosity may know no bounds right now, so consider leaving the credit cards at home. Interactions with females tend to be lucky for you. Listen to the advice of one of them in regard to a money matter. There can be wisdom in her words.

Weekly Summary

Your intuition seems to be on target right now. If you follow your hunches, you may find that you just happen to be in the right place at the right time. This situation can provide you with a chance to earn a lot of money. Keep an eye on activities going on behind the scenes at work right now. There can be something there that you need to investigate.

You can be provided with an opportunity to dazzle other people when you are invited to a very exclusive social affair at this time. Check your wardrobe ahead of time. This situation may warrant a shopping spree, and the investment will be worth it. You can make one or two very important contacts when there, both socially and romantically.

It may be time to pay serious attention to a money drain this week. It would have been easier to avoid dealing with it earlier, but that may no longer be a feasible option. Deal with it now before it becomes a real liability. This may involve developing more discipline and structure, both of which you should have in abundance at this time.

4th Week/January 22–28

Wednesday the 22nd. Your efforts should pay off in the form of a financial reward. You will feel better now that a business transaction has been negotiated and completed to your satisfaction. You are able to deal with details patiently now, so this can be a good time to edit reports for errors or to do some number crunching.

Thursday the 23rd. The people around you can be in a social mood, so take time to stop to chat with those whom you bump into. This can be a good time to have a talk with a close friend about a serious subject, as you can both remain objective. You tend to be on the move today, possibly embarking on a short road trip.

Friday the 24th. Disruptions in communications may keep you on your toes. Computers can go down unexpectedly, so be sure to back up any important documents. Traffic tie-ups are likely to cause delays, so don't be surprised if an appointment is late or even fails to show up at all. Try to remain flexible and allow extra travel time.

Saturday the 25th. A romantic relationship can get more intense. Your love interest may be feeling insecure at the moment and therefore come across as overly controlling. Reassure your love of your intentions. You may find yourself being pressured into a financial deal due to time constraints. Exercise your better judgment. Take all the time that you think you need.

Sunday the 26th. This can be a good time to select new furnishings or appliances for your home. Invest in things that add an element of warmth and comfort. A family gathering can work out well. Make it a potluck so that other people can bring favorite food, giving you more time to enjoy your family.

Monday the 27th. You are in an adventurous mood. Staying pinned down to one spot can be difficult now, so volunteer to take a business trip that is up for grabs. Some man from your past may make an appearance. He is likely to want something from you now, so be suspicious of his motives. Get outside for some fresh air and exercise.

Tuesday the 28th. You may be feeling some disappointment in a love relationship. Your partner may not be fulfilling your expectations in some way. Decide if your bottom-line needs are being met or not, and speak out. A child may be a handful this evening, perhaps experiencing some growing pains. Allow the youngster some breathing room now.

Weekly Summary

You probably are feeling more restless than usual this week. Guard against starting too many different things and then not finishing them. Instead of trying to make yourself buckle down, consider taking off on a short trip to visit some pals. It could be fun, and provide the kind of distraction and stimulation that you may need right now.

Your security may be on your mind, both economically and emotionally. Be receptive to the ideas of a relative. A family member may be a connection to a lucrative business or financial contact. Allow a meeting to be set up, as it can help to boost you up the ladder of success.

You are likely to be in the mood for some fun. Let your hair down and kick up your heels with some good friends. Go to a party, or throw one yourself. You can appreciate good entertainment as well. Attend a performance of live theater, or have a good laugh at a comedy show. Others prefer to follow your lead now, so you may be in charge of getting the tickets.

5th Week/January 29–February 4

Wednesday the 29th. You may be an expert at managing details right now. Deal with bills, balance your checkbook, and make any necessary appointments for yourself or the kids. An older relative may need your assistance in some way this afternoon. Offer your help, but don't take on the problems of others as your own. Retire early and get a good night's sleep.

Thursday the 30th. Whatever you begin now will probably last for a long time. This should be a good time to make investments or to buy a house that you want to live in for years to come. Avoid starting anything that requires a quick turnover. Take care of routine tasks and chores. Stock up on your vitamins at the health food store.

Friday the 31st. A relationship can show some promise of becoming more serious. This may depend on your ability to show how reliable and dependable you are now. Make the effort, and you will be glad that you did. Spend the evening catching up with a group of old friends. An impromptu get-together promises to be fun, as well as informative.

Saturday February 1st. You may be involved in some conflict negotiations, and your ability to remain detached and clear can enable you to come to an equitable solution. This can be a good time to let go of things that are just adding clutter to your life. It may also be time to let go of the people who may be holding you back.

Sunday the 2nd. Anything that you begin now should show signs of success within the month. This can be a good time to join a health or social club, or to make a new friend. Your romantic life probably will pick up. Someone that you meet through a friend this afternoon may turn out to be quite wonderful. Make an effort to find out.

Monday the 3rd. You may be concerned about expenses. More of your money may be flowing out than there is coming in right now. A solution may be imminent, and you have the motivation and discipline to put it into effect. The boss may now be more approachable than usual, so this could be a good time to ask for a raise.

Tuesday the 4th. It may be more difficult than usual to buckle down to work. You may be inclined to dream and drift right now. Use your talents of visualization in a creative project instead. Your compassionate side can come out now when a stray animal shows up on your doorstep this evening. Maybe it's time for a new pet.

Weekly Summary

An elderly relative may need your support right now. Make an effort to help out as best as you can. Even a visit can make a world of difference to the mental attitude of a shut-in. You can help by taking care of errands, shopping, and doing various other chores around the house. Take care of your health right now by eating well and getting lots of sleep.

You and your partner seem to be on an upswing in your relationship right now. Take a second honeymoon and enjoy each other. If things aren't quite that rosy, they soon will be. It may be your busy schedules that have interfered with your time alone. Make an effort to get away together, and the passion should soon be reignited.

An investment opportunity may come your way via close friends or relatives. Don't let anyone's obvious enthusiasm sway your own good judgment, however. Do some investigating and get some background information. It may be too risky a venture for you at this time. Thank people, but don't feel guilty. It's your money after all.

6th Week/February 5–11

Wednesday the 5th. Your energy level can be quite high now. You may be having an adrenaline rush, so pursue competitive sports or an endeavor requiring lots of physical movement. Big ideas and big plans may be dominating your thoughts right now. Consult a smart friend to get some practical input, however. Together you may be able to make your ideas workable.

Thursday the 6th. Your powers of persuasion are higher than usual. This should hold you in good stead when dealing with clients or with salespeople. Your sense of humor can get you through almost anything at this time. A potential conflict with a colleague can be averted by your ability to see the light side of things.

Friday the 7th. Travel may be on the agenda. You may be planning a big trip abroad or setting off to visit some pals for the weekend. Either way, a change of scenery is likely to be just what you need right now. Someone may push your buttons by unwanted advice. State firmly that your opinion is the only one that fits for you.

Saturday the 8th. You may find yourself thrust into the spotlight in some way. You may be the winner of an athletic event, or you may be the guest of honor at some sort of celebration. Soak up the applause. You deserve it. Treat yourself well this evening. Luxuriate in a gourmet dinner with fine wine and pleasant and appreciative company.

Sunday the 9th. Your physical senses will be more acute than usual. Treat yourself to a massage or a facial this afternoon. Working with your hands can bring on a sense of satisfaction. Work on a crafts project, do some carpentry, or knead some bread dough. The last suggestion is likely to be the family's favorite.

Monday the 10th. You should be efficient and productive now. A need for variety can make it difficult to stick with one thing for an extended period of time, however. Compromise by working on a project that allows for movement and variety within it. Efforts made to communicate with an estranged friend or relative should be reciprocated at this time.

Tuesday the 11th. This can be an auspicious time to engage in verbal exchanges and negotiations. You can finesse the finer points of a contract to your benefit now. Verbal or written reports given to the boss or to colleagues should make an impression. You may be required to field questions from your audience, so be ready with the supporting data.

Weekly Summary

You may be wanting to break away from the routine of everyday life for a while. Take a little time off and do something completely different and unusual. Go on a road trip to someplace new. Take off and visit some friends you haven't seen in a long time, or join a tour group and go on the adventure of a lifetime.

You may be reconsidering your future goals and ambitions at this time. Something exciting and new may have popped up unexpectedly, inspiring you with new ideas. Consider following this new road and see where it takes you. Perhaps you have uncovered a new passion, one that could be your passion for life. Give it due time and consideration.

Your social circle can be in the process of expansion this week. Joining a new club or association can put you in contact with a wide variety of people. This should be a very auspicious time to go to parties and various other social get-togethers. A romantic association may be one of the results.

7th Week/February 12–18

Wednesday the 12th. You will want to keep things lighthearted and breezy now. Heavy conversations may best be left for another time. Call up a friend you haven't seen in a while and make some plans. You may learn you have been missed. Consider donating time in lieu of cash to a humanitarian organization when it asks for your help.

Thursday the 13th. A situation with a relative can be resolved amicably, but you may need to initiate the interaction. If you set the tone, people are likely to follow your lead. Invest in home furnishings. Comfort seems to be a priority at this time, so consider splurging on something that makes you want to curl up and relax.

Friday the 14th. Home entertainment can be a high point of your day. You are proud of your home and may want to share its comfort with friends and family right now. The Moon in Leo may bring a new romance into your life this Valentine's Day. Prepare a delicious meal for your newest heartthrob.

Saturday the 15th. Things should be going your way. All you really need to do is to show up. You have incredible powers of focus and discipline at this time. Channel them into something that has meaning for you. Creative pursuits can be profitable for you. You may find a way to turn a hobby into a lucrative source of income.

Sunday the 16th. Tensions may be running higher than usual in yourself as well as in everyone around you. Avoid direct confrontation at this time. Wait until you are in a calmer and more lucid state of mind. Your emotions may get the better of you now, and you can say something in the heat of the moment that you will regret at a later date.

Monday the 17th. This can be an incredibly lucky day for you romantically. Someone that you first lay eyes on now can be in your life for a very long time. This person may not be your usual type. If you already have a partner, go with some changes that are going on in your personal life. They should ultimately be in your best interest.

Tuesday the 18th. It may feel as if the whole world is against you, when it may actually be your own doubts that are getting the best of you right now. Don't let the jibes of a jealous colleague affect your self-confidence. Realize that you do have the ability and the talent that is needed to get the job done right.

Weekly Summary

You may find that you prefer to operate from behind the scenes this week. Although being in the spotlight is usually your preference, that position is not likely to work well for you right now. You need some private time to think things through and to plan your strategy without distraction. You should emerge from this solitude with more confidence than ever.

You find that you work best independently this week. Cooperation with others may be more difficult than usual now, so save yourself the time and the aggravation of even trying. Set personal projects into motion. Don't wait for the approval of other people. Do what feels right for you, on your own schedule. You can thus chase away any lingering doubts about your abilities.

Money matters may need to be taken care of immediately. Although you abhor budgeting in any form, it may be necessary in order to keep yourself in the lifestyle you desire for a long time to come. A little bit of sacrifice now will pay off later. Consider asking a professional for some advice.

8th Week/February 19–25

Wednesday the 19th. You may be suffering from information overload right now. Staying organized will probably be your key to success. Although you may be tempted to take on everything at once, try to remain focused on one or two things instead. Scattering your energies can only result in projects not being completed to your high standards of excellence.

Thursday the 20th. You can get excited by new ideas. Seeing the potential in the plan of a colleague may make you want to take some practical steps to implement it. You should make a successful team if you decide to work together. You appreciate beauty in all of its forms now. Visit an art gallery this afternoon.

Friday the 21st. Your mind is quick and insightful just now. A friend may not be lying to you, but may be holding something back. Interrogate the person further to get the full story. Love can be intense and passionate at this time. If you are single, an attraction to someone can make some progress this evening.

Saturday the 22nd. You probably are involved in financial dealings. This can be an auspicious time to invest in large-ticket items, such as home furnishings or pieces of collectible art. Your mate may come into some unexpected money at this time. It can come from a commission, a repaid debt, or a winning lottery ticket.

Sunday the 23rd. You may be out on the road, heading for adventure. Take a friend along. If getting away is a problem, immerse yourself in something that inspires you this afternoon. Work on a pet project, or consider starting a new hobby of some sort. Talking philosophy with a good friend or partner can make for a pleasant evening.

Monday the 24th. You may surprise yourself by playing the role of teacher. Leading a seminar at work, or perhaps showing the new guy the ropes can be on the agenda. Either way, you can inspire others as you instruct them now. Try to hold your own counsel with relatives this evening, even if it means having to watch them make their own mistakes.

Tuesday the 25th. You can make your mark through some sort of accomplishment. Accept kudos from others and bask in your well-earned glory. Avoid being too rigid when dealing with employees or co-workers this afternoon. Support their efforts, however unconventional they may be. Physical exercise is important for your physical and mental well-being now. Go for a long walk after dinner.

Weekly Summary

An upcoming trip will have you all excited. Now is the time to take care of loose ends at work, clearing the decks before you go. You will be quite busy and on the go this week. Avoid taking on anything new. Leaving unfinished business behind will cause unnecessary worry while you are away. Getting away from it all should be your main concern now.

This can be a good time to do some home entertaining. You can impress the boss by inviting him or her over for a home-cooked meal. Break out the good china and be sure to invest in a really good bottle of wine. Consider getting together with chums one night this week. A potluck dinner can allow everyone to get involved and reduce your own work load as well.

You and your best friend are likely to be really active right now. Getting out and enjoying life depends on where you are. You may want to dress up and hit the town one night, and then dress down and go to an amusement park another.

9th Week/February 26–March 4

Wednesday the 26th. A job offer can come your way through a client who is impressed with your work. Consider taking on the challenge, especially if more money or more authority is involved. An older colleague may give you some patronizing, yet well-meaning, advice this afternoon. Be polite, but let the individual know that a personal boundary has been crossed.

Thursday the 27th. Your tendency is to be ambitious and hard-working. Productive and efficient, you are not inclined to waste time chatting or socializing now. This should be a good time to tackle any project that may have seemed overwhelming before. A money matter can be discussed calmly with a mate this evening. You should come to a meeting of the minds.

Friday the 28th. You are in a very sociable frame of mind. Friendship is quite important to you now, and your efforts on behalf of a good friend will be noticed and gratefully received. This can be a good time for group activities. Join a health club or a local social club.

Saturday March 1st. You may attend a trade show or a conference related to your profession. Interaction with other people can inspire you now, helping you to come up with new ideas. You can communicate well on a larger or more humanitarian level, but you may not feel comfortable having an intimate or heart-to-heart talk with a loved one under present circumstances.

Sunday the 2nd. This should be a good day for new beginnings. It may require letting go of certain habits or of certain people who are no longer good for you. Once done, you will feel more free, with a greater sense of power. This can be a good day to introduce a new pet to the family. You can find one at the local animal shelter.

Monday the 3rd. Your energy level can be higher than usual. Find a constructive outlet and go for it. Physical endeavors are favored at this time. Consider participating in a recreational volleyball league, or attend a martial arts class. An elderly relative may be missing you right now. Make plans for a visit very soon.

Tuesday the 4th. You may be renegotiating an alliance of some sort. This can be with your lawyer, your business partner, or even your current love interest. Don't be afraid to state exactly what you want and expect. A need for speed can cause you to be more impatient than usual. Avoid traffic jams now to save yourself the aggravation.

Weekly Summary

Your work ethic may be very strong at this time. You are likely to get much satisfaction from a job well done. Take care of routine tasks and chores. Your attention to detail now should help you to deal with tasks you may have previously avoided. In regard to work, one project in particular may not be ready to be put away yet. There still can be some more fine-tuning needed.

Your primary romantic relationship is probably at the top of your list of priorities right now. You may be in the process of figuring out how much time to spend together. You may want your space, but not at the expense of your love life. This can be the perfect time to sit down with your partner to discuss your mutual expectations and needs.

You or your partner can be on the receiving end of some money at this time, perhaps through commissions or benefits. Some of you may get a large tax refund or perhaps an inheritance from a long-lost relative. This also is a good time to deal with credit card bills or any other accrued debt.

10th Week/March 5–11

Wednesday the 5th. You can experience an urge for freedom. Being pinned down feels uncomfortable now. A short road trip can help to change your perspective. If you have the time, consider taking an extended vacation. Learning something new can stimulate you mentally. Consider signing up for a class at night school or a local library.

Thursday the 6th. You may find yourself involved in some sort of legal proceeding, which can involve jury duty or even a court case of your own. Things will work out in your favor in the long run if you can be patient. You can promote yourself or your business more effectively than usual now. Attend a business-related social event this evening to make contacts.

Friday the 7th. You will attract many admiring glances as others react to your regal bearing and natural charm. You may even find yourself in the spotlight in some way, perhaps accepting an honor for a special kind of accomplishment. Go out and celebrate with close friends and loved ones. Make a point of living up to the expectations of a child this evening.

Saturday the 8th. You are in the mood to experience the best that life has to offer now. There may be no cutting corners with you, as you insist on investing in quality clothing and entertainment. Only front row center tickets may do, as well as the finest in wine and dining. Others can learn from your ability to live life to the fullest.

Sunday the 9th. The phone is likely to be ringing off the hook, bringing invitations from friends. Social interactions should keep you busy and fulfilled at this time, but guard against spreading yourself too thin. Keep an eye on your pocketbook now, as impulse spending may cause you to buy now and regret later. Stock up on your supply of reading material.

Monday the 10th. You are looked on as communicative and witty. Avoid getting pulled into a power play at the office, however. A colleague may try to sweet-talk you into seeing things his way, but he may not be telling you the whole truth. Time spent with younger people can ensure your good mood and also keep you on your toes.

Tuesday the 11th. A decision you made about a week ago can be up for renegotiation now. It may still be a good choice, but some minor adjustments may be necessary. A problem in your love life can be ironed out more easily at this time if you make a point of sitting down and talking about it. Avoidance can only exacerbate the problem.

Weekly Summary

You probably will be wanting to get away from it all right now, and a few days off may not be enough. Consider using a large chunk of your vacation time and going on an extended holiday. This can be a good time to broaden your horizons and to expand your perspective on life. You will be able to find new inspiration in your travels and can return home completely rejuvenated.

A job offer may come your way out of the blue. This opportunity is likely to entail doing something that is completely different from what you are presently doing, but consider taking on this challenge, especially if you have been looking to expand your career horizons.

This new job can lead to even bigger and better things in the future.

You perhaps will be giving serious thought to becoming involved in community and local affairs. Your natural charm and leadership abilities will make you the perfect candidate to lead rallies or to organize current charity drives. People can draw strength from your confident attitude.

11th Week/March 12–18

Wednesday the 12th. Part of you may want to daydream, but circumstances may prevent it from happening. You probably will be called upon to accept some sort of responsibility now, thus making it difficult to stay in a reverie. Romance this evening can be idyllic, however. Make a point of planning something special and wonderful for you and your love.

Thursday the 13th. Fulfilling domestic obligations may take up some of your morning. You enjoy staying close to home right now. Baking, cooking, and tending to your nest should provide satisfaction at this time. You may require more private time than you normally do. Pick up a good novel or video this evening and cozy up alone or with a loved one.

Friday the 14th. Things seem to go naturally your way. Take advantage of the Moon's presence in Leo to ask important people for important favors. You should get noticed now, even more than you usually do. For double impact, dress for success and make an entrance wherever you go. You are quite comfortable taking the lead in making plans this evening.

Saturday the 15th. You may want to be free to pursue your own projects this weekend. You will be better off being noncommittal when approached with possible plans for this evening. Just go with the flow and see how you feel as you go along. Being pinned down to any one thing can make you feel uncomfortable right now.

Sunday the 16th. You are feeling very industrious now. You can get much accomplished around the house this morning if you get up early. Your efficiency and productivity may even inspire other household members to pitch in. Efforts made to improve your health and diet should pay off. Be sure to get some exercise, and stock up on your vitamin supply.

Monday the 17th. You may need to fine-tune plans before moving ahead with them in a practical way. Don't let your enthusiasm and impatience cause you to jump ahead before you are ready. Avoid being too critical of a colleague or co-worker at this time. Even though you may not understand the individual's point of view, it is still likely to have value.

Tuesday the 18th. Tensions can be running higher than usual in those around you as well as in yourself. Your primary relationship may be going through some growing pains now. This should be an excellent time to deal with the issues, gaining more clarity into what each of you needs and wants. Make time for the two of you to be alone.

Weekly Summary

You will possibly be wanting more private time. Being in the spotlight may not be where you feel most comfortable at this time. Don't feel bad declining an invitation to a party or to a social affair connected with work. You will reap more benefits by staying in the background now, recharging your batteries.

You will be ready to take on the world now, after taking a little rest for yourself. Your mind seems to be clear and focused, and you should be ready to tackle anything that comes your way. This can be a good time to take practical steps to put project plans into motion. Consider taking on a partner whose knowledge complements your own.

This is an auspicious time to take care of financial matters. Setting up a budget can be a good way to take stock of what comes in and what goes out. There may be a larger discrepancy there than you thought. Avoid being too stringent in your budget, however. Be sure to allow some room for the occasional indulgence.

12th Week/March 19–25

Wednesday the 19th. You will be out and around for most of the day, running errands and keeping appointments. Be prepared to stop and chat along the way, as people seem to be very socially oriented at this time. You really appreciate beauty in all of its forms right now. Redecorate your home, or invest in some artwork.

Thursday the 20th. You may want to stay close to home just now. You can appreciate some quiet time, so avoid overbooking yourself with appointments. A lost item may be a cause of concern because of its sentimental value. Look in places that are low, dark, or damp. You might find it under the couch, in the basement, or close to a water source.

Friday the 21st. You may find that you have an enhanced need to communicate. This should be a good time to have a heart-to-heart talk with a loved one, as you can get to the core of any problems right now. You can benefit from current low-risk investments. You may stand to make a tidy sum over the long haul as a result.

Saturday the 22nd. You want to be in control of things. This may not work to your advantage right now, however, as it could entail doing everything yourself. Try to develop an attitude of trust in others instead. You may be pleasantly surprised with the results. A low-key evening may be on the agenda. Enjoy a dinner out with close friends.

Sunday the 23rd. You can expect to be in a very optimistic and playful mood. Get out and enjoy the day with friends or a loved one. Hiking, biking, or skiing should all satisfy your thirst for adventure at this time. Being pinned down to one location is likely to make you antsy right now, so consider taking a short road trip with a family member.

Monday the 24th. You probably will be up and at work early this morning. Your energy levels are high now, but your initial burst of enthusiasm may be as short-lived as your attention span. Allow yourself some variety in what you do. Short-term goals can provide the motivation for you to succeed right now.

Tuesday the 25th. You seem to have the gift of gab at present. You can inspire others with your ideas, so this should be a good time to give a speech or to teach a class. Your public image is likely to be an important consideration for you at this time. This should be a good day to shop for career clothing.

Weekly Summary

You may be in the market for a new car, stereo, or computer at this time. Considerable savings can be had if you take the time to do your homework. Check out consumer reports via the Internet, or log on and read what other buyers have to say. Once armed with the necessary information, you should be able to make the best possible deal.

Sprucing up your domestic environment will be fun for you this week. This can be a good time to buy new furniture or to rearrange your existing furniture for a whole new look. Add a few new colorful cushions or consider painting the walls a different color. Even little changes can make a world of difference in how you feel.

Your creative side can be clamoring to take over at this time. Allow it free rein by trying something artistic. Take a sculpting class or try to learn to play an instrument. Do some finger painting with the kids, and you may surprise yourself with how much you enjoy it. Consider making a friend's birthday gift instead of buying it. The recipient will be honored by your efforts.

13th Week/March 26–April 1

Wednesday the 26th. An unexpected job opportunity may come your way. It will be worth taking it just for the experience, even if the wage is lower than you might want right now. An older man may need your assistance in some way. Let him know that you are available to help out in any way that you can.

Thursday the 27th. Friendships can be the most important part of the day for you. One friendship in particular may be undergoing changes. If platonic, it could turn romantic. Stay open to the possibilities. This will be a good time to join a new group of some sort. A health club or hobby group may provide you with opportunities to expand your social circle.

Friday the 28th. This can be a very auspicious day on all fronts. Whatever you do now will be met with success. Your love life may take a turn for the better as well. Someone you meet now can make your heart go pitter-patter, but avoid jumping in too fast. Start slow, and you will have a better chance of making it work.

Saturday the 29th. You are feeling quite compassionate this weekend. Others are drawn to you now for some friendly advice. Avoid taking on the problems of friends, however. Remain detached, yet show you care. This can be a good time to introduce a new pet to the family. You can look forward to escaping into a good movie or novel this evening.

Sunday the 30th. You may prefer to lie low at present. Reflection and meditation can be what gives you the most pleasure at this time. Avoid putting any pressure on yourself. If possible, try to get away to the mountains or the ocean for some fresh air and beautiful scenery. A loved one may ask you to let him or her come along.

Monday the 31st. Conversations tend to be serious and in-depth. Superficial interactions will only bore you now. Spend time around people who provide you with inspiration while avoiding those who bring you down. Writers and artists may find that they are producing excellent work. Use the creative side of your brain this evening on an arts and crafts project.

Tuesday April 1st. You can see the results of projects begun now sooner than you expect. This is an especially good time to strike out on your own in some way. You should find that independent action gets supported by others now. A new sport begun at this time may end up becoming a lifelong passion. Be patient through the learning process though.

Weekly Summary

You will find that exerting discipline is easier than usual this week. This can be an auspicious time to drop an old habit and to replace it with a new and healthier one. You are happiest when you are busy and feeling useful. Take advantage of this industrious attitude to clean out closets, drawers, and filing cabinets.

You may be involved in negotiating a very important deal with another party at this time. Although you are eager to finalize things, avoid sacrificing your own needs and wants in order to expedite matters. Slow down and take your time. Analyze the fine print. Ask the opinion of a savvy friend. The more time you take and the more input you get, the better satisfied you will be with the outcome.

You may come into some money at this time. This unexpected pay-off can arrive in the form of a loan repayment from a friend. You may have written off this debt a long time ago, making it that much more satisfying to receive now. Treat yourself to something wonderful.

14th Week/April 2–8

Wednesday the 2nd. You may seem larger than life to others just now. Your apparent confidence can inspire others to take notice of what you say and of what you do. Take advantage of being in the spotlight this way by exceeding integrity and compassion. You can make a difference. Channel any excess energy by taking a long walk this evening by the water.

Thursday the 3rd. You are sure to appreciate the little luxuries in life now. Don't deny yourself completely. Indulge in a beautiful item of clothing that you adore, or go out to a scrumptious dinner that you and a companion can appreciate together. It can be so much the better if you are called upon to entertain a client for business; then you can write everything off.

Friday the 4th. The boss may ask you to take on some extra responsibilities. This may provide you with a good chance to win some big points, but be sure that you are getting financially compensated as well. No one is likely to respect your giving away your time for free. Accept an invitation to a friend's house for dinner tonight.

Saturday the 5th. You have the gift of being able to focus at present. Being persistent will ensure that you get the results that you want. Avoid bossing other people around in the process, however. Using tact and diplomacy will work better for you now. Setting up a home-based business can be the start of something big.

Sunday the 6th. You may consider attending a trade show or a charity fund-raiser. Being with like-minded people is always important to you. Expect to meet someone special at one of these functions. You may find that you have much in common. If you are single, a romance may ensue, but you may become good friends first.

Monday the 7th. You are almost sure to interact with a wide variety of people. Make a point of listening more than talking right now. Vital information may come your way, so be on the alert for it. An old friend may ask for a favor. Decide if this friend is one who exhibits the kind of loyalty that you currently require.

Tuesday the 8th. You want to feel secure these days. Sticking close to home can be one way to accomplish that. If you have to be out and around, stick to a routine that you are familiar with. This can be a good time to renew a connection with a family member that you may not have seen for a while.

Weekly Summary

You may be interacting with people from afar right now. A business deal can put you in touch with some international contacts. Some traveling may be involved in this situation, so be ready to take off without much notice. A traveling friend can get in touch with you as well, suggesting a meeting at some exotic place.

You can make a good first impression this week. Job interviews can go well now, as do consultations and meetings with bigwigs. Your confident air and charming manner can sway even the most stalwart of opponents. This is likely to be a good time for creative types to display their work in a public building.

Working on behalf of a humanitarian group or civil rights effort may be a good way to broaden your horizons right now. You will find that your social circle expands to include some new and different types of people as a result. Your old friends may still be important to you, but it is vital to recognize that your values may be changing.

15th Week/April 9–15

Wednesday the 9th. You may be rethinking a decision made about one week ago. New information can come to light, causing you to reassess matters. Remember that you have the right to change your mind, regardless of what someone else thinks. Take time out for yourself this evening. Curl up with a good book, or cook a yummy dinner.

Thursday the 10th. You are more inclined than usual toward sentimentality. Spend time with loved ones now, as you can appreciate what they bring to your life. If you are single, you can start a romance with someone with whom you can envision yourself settling down. This person is quite witty and fun, yet gentle and kind as well. Lucky you.

Friday the 11th. Things just seem to go your way at present. This may be a good time to go out and make things happen. You can win big financially, as well as romantically now. Self-expression is your key to success. Put out what you want, and others will accommodate your request. You can make important contacts tonight.

Saturday the 12th. You may need to find a constructive outlet for your considerable energy. This can help to prevent you from getting annoyed and irritated at the little things. Focus on a project that requires discipline and effort. Bodybuilders should get good results now, as should anyone exerting effort toward a goal. Entertain yourself with some high drama this evening.

Sunday the 13th. You want perfection now, and you are prepared to exert much effort in order to achieve this standard. Try to let go, and allow good enough to be good enough. It may be easier than usual to find fault with a loved one. Try to focus on good qualities instead of faults. Remember that you have faults too.

Monday the 14th. Money matters can be on your mind just now. This can be a good time to balance the checkbook and to take a look at the budget. A few adjustments may be necessary in order to better reflect your current financial needs. Cleaning and organizing around the house can help you to feel calm and secure all day long.

Tuesday the 15th. You seem to be in quite a social frame of mind. Take time to chat with colleagues and catch up on the office grapevine over an extended lunch hour. Expect friends to call you up now. You and a partner may enjoy spending some quality time together this evening. Communication between you is enhanced and harmonious.

Weekly Summary

Take some time to recharge your batteries this week. You may have been playing as hard as you have been working lately. Burning out will not benefit anyone else, let alone yourself. Consider a complete change of scenery. Taking a few days to get away to the mountains or to the seaside can do a world of good for your mental and physical disposition right now.

You may be thinking that it's your way or the highway at this time. Compromising with others may not be easy for you. On the other hand, this can be a great time to forge ahead with independent projects and plans. You have the necessary confidence and optimism to succeed in whatever you put your mind to.

This can be a good time to go over your financial

portfolio and make any necessary reassessments. It may be that your financial goals have changed somewhat recently. Don't hesitate to invest in things that better reflect your current status and desires. A professional may be able to offer some sage advice in this area.

16th Week/April 16–22

Wednesday the 16th. Issues in a relationship may come to a head, which is likely to be a good thing. It should result in greater clarity about where you stand with each other. Take a day or two to think about things before making any decisions, however. Beware of a financial deal that looks too good to be true.

Thursday the 17th. People around you may be emotionally volatile, and your temper may be challenged as well. Some Leos will channel their energy into Passover observances. Others may actively pursue a pet project. This can be an especially good time to engage in anything competitive, but remember to be a good sport even if you don't win.

Friday the 18th. Domestic concerns can be part of the day's scenario. It may be time to have a little talk with other household members; make sure that everyone pitches in with chores. You can be given the green light to buy or sell a house. Those of you who are looking to rent an apartment can have good luck this afternoon.

Saturday the 19th. You probably will be taking part in some sort of celebration. You may be attending a graduation, a wedding, or a class or family reunion. Don't be surprised if you run into an old flame from the past.

The old spark may still be there, but withhold judgment on whether the person has really changed.

Sunday the 20th. Fun and adventure are likely to be calling your name this Easter Sunday. Forgo your usual routine and do something exciting with your mate. If you are single, join friends on a bike ride or mountain hike. Whatever you do, be sure to get outside into the fresh air for a while. A good game of chess, checkers, or Monopoly can make for a fun evening.

Monday the 21st. You are in a no-nonsense frame of mind. Expect to be quite productive and efficient as a result. More work may be needed on a pet project. Review it before submission to make sure that it is up to your high standards. If looking for a new job, follow up on a tip from a female friend.

Tuesday the 22nd. Expect the unexpected, especially around the workplace. Your office space may be changing, or you may need to accommodate new staff in some way. Roll with the punches now, and you should adjust to the changes soon enough. A female friend can impress you with her staunch loyalty toward you at this time. Let her know how you feel.

Weekly Summary

You may find this week that new neighbors have moved in very close to you. This can be a good opportunity to set a positive and considerate tone between you. Take the initiative. Bake some cookies and take them over on a welcome-to-the-neighborhood visit. Once the people are aware of you personally, they are more likely to be considerate of you in the matter of noise.

This can be an auspicious time to invest money and time in your domestic environment. Redecorating a room or two should add color and light to your dwelling place. Using valuable art to add elegance and beauty to your home can also be seen as a smart financial investment. Comfort and beauty are equally important to you at this time.

You are in the mood to play right now. Games of chance and amusement park rides can be loads of fun. Take the kids along and delight in their excitement as well. Games that require a certain amount of intelligence may be to your liking now. Try your hand at chess, or challenge yourself with logic puzzles.

17th Week/April 23–29

Wednesday the 23rd. Your primary relationship will be a focus for you. Tempers can flare up easily at this time. Try to nip a minor conflict in the bud before it escalates into an even bigger one. Channeling any excess energy between you into a competitive sport or physical activity of some kind can help to transmute it.

Thursday the 24th. You probably are working in tandem with a partner on a project. Sit back and let the other person take the lead for a change. You might even enjoy it. You may be approached by a charity organization to make a donation. Consider offering to do some work in lieu of cash. Getting involved can expand your social circle immensely.

Friday the 25th. You are likely to exhibit an air of detached optimism. Nothing much gets to you now. This can be a good time to negotiate and resolve a conflict with a friend, as you should be able to stay clear and calm in the process. Accept an invitation to a party this evening and be prepared to have some fun.

Saturday the 26th. Finances can be on your mind. Take care of mortgage or credit card bills now, before any undue interest is accumulated. A check in the mail will be a pleasant and timely surprise right now. You may receive a tax return or unexpected insurance benefit of some sort. A party this evening promises to be entertaining.

Sunday the 27th. Confusion will upset your best-laid plans. Be sure to back up any important documents on your computer just in case. Leave early when you travel; traffic snarls can cause some major delays. Don't be surprised if people you are meeting fail to show up. Reconfirm all appointment times before leaving home. Your best bet may be to remain flexible.

Monday the 28th. Your obvious enthusiasm will be contagious. People will be attracted to your zest for life at this time. If you are single, an admirer may make himself or herself known to you. This person may be athletic and fun-loving. Although your first instinct is to jump in head-first, allow yourself time to get to know the individual first.

Tuesday the 29th. You have big dreams now and may set your sights very high. Try to be realistic in order to prevent disappointment, however. Travel plans may be on the agenda. The boss may ask you to take off for places unknown for business reasons. Try to squeeze in a few days for fun as well.

Weekly Summary

You will want to improve your diet and health regimen this week. Time, or lack of it, probably is the vital factor that is holding you back. Planning ahead may be the strategy that works for you now. Stock up on healthy fruits and vegetables that you can snack on at a moment's notice. Preplanned meals can cut preparation time in half.

You may be deciding whether or not to take on a friend as a business partner right now. Your skills may complement each other, rendering your success more easily attainable; but be wary of the friendship factor. Keep it safe by getting clear on your mutual goals and methods of reaching them. Ground rules laid out at the beginning can be a good idea as well.

Get out old insurance policies and warranties to make sure that everything is up to date. You may want to add to your household insurance to better reflect the value of your possessions at this time. You may be able to get a computer or an appliance fixed under warranty if you take care of it right away.

18th Week/April 30–May 6

Wednesday the 30th. You can successfully promote yourself right now. Your belief in yourself or your work can be enough to sway just about anybody. This can be a good time to invest in advertising, as reaching an international audience may be your key to success at this time. Foreigners tend to be lucky for you, and you may find yourself in contact with a few.

Thursday May 1st. Start something now, and you will achieve success within the month. This can be an especially good time to make a new financial deal, to plant a new garden, or to enroll in a cooking class. Things that require you to use your physical senses are important at this time. You should especially enjoy a massage now.

Friday the 2nd. Your career efforts can pay off now. You may be thrust into the spotlight in some way for a job well done. Accept your kudos graciously. A promotion or pay raise can be part of the scenario as well. Your love life may kick into high gear this evening. Attend a party thrown by a colleague.

Saturday the 3rd. You may be prone to seeing things the way that you wish they were. Try to stay grounded and realistic. It can be easy to make false assumptions about people or situations now, especially when you are not given all of the pertinent information. Stay on your toes, and question everything that comes your way.

Sunday the 4th. Spend the day with a close friend whom you have not seen in a while. That individual may be thinking about you as well, wondering where you have been. Resolve to stay in closer contact. Expect to communicate with a wide variety of people now. Friends are more likely to drop in unannounced · at this time, so be prepared.

Monday the 5th. Perhaps you will find yourself taking part in a group event. This may be a charity fund-raiser of some sort, or even a political rally. Your leadership abilities can be a wonderful asset to the team, so consider offering them. You enjoy being busy now, but avoid taking on too many projects all at once.

Tuesday the 6th. You will find that you prefer to stay behind the scenes at present. This position can help you to strategize and to plot your next move without interruption. You and your mate may disagree on an important issue. Support each other's point of view instead of trying to change each other's mind. A compromise may be easier as a result.

Weekly Summary

You may be eager to break out of your routine this week. Being pinned down to one place can be very difficult to bear right now, so it can be prime time for travel. Take your vacation time to head to someplace foreign and exciting. Experiencing a new and different culture can help to broaden your perspective, perhaps resulting in some new goals and ambitions for your future.

You may be reaping the fruits of your labors now. Any efforts that you have made toward furthering your career should be paying off with attention from higherups. Creative types may find interested buyers for their work, and corporate types are in high demand right now. Personal satisfaction can be its own reward now as well.

You may get the chance to become more active in community affairs this week. Helping to organize a walkathon for charity should bring a sense of satisfaction, as would heading up a political rally for a candidate in whom you believe. Express yourself in the community, and a whole new world will open up before you.

19th Week/May 7–13

Wednesday the 7th. You are more security-minded than usual. A financial investment made now will perform very well over the long haul, especially if it involves communications or technology in some form. This can be a very good time to open a home-based business, even if it is just a small one to make some extra cash on the side.

Thursday the 8th. Lady Luck is on your side, so don't hesitate to take a calculated risk or two. You attract attention wherever you go now, so dress your best. You never know whom you may bump into. A male friend may try to recruit you for his latest escapade. Be sure to get the facts straight before committing yourself either way.

Friday the 9th. Those plans you made last Friday may not be working out exactly as expected. See this minor glitch as a universal gift, as it may make you aware of something that you otherwise would not have known about. A romantic partner may lavish some extra love and attention on you now. Let him or her take the lead in making plans for the evening.

Saturday the 10th. Financial matters may take precedence this morning. Get all your accounting done and make a quick scan of the budget to make sure that things are going according to plan. If you don't have a budget, consider making one at this time. You may be surprised when you see exactly how much is coming in compared to how much is going out.

Sunday the 11th. Communications with others may be subject to misinterpretation. Be sure to say exactly what you mean in order to avoid mix-ups. Tackle household chores and routine tasks this afternoon. Enlist the aid of other family members, and delegate where necessary. You will be in the mood for activity this evening. Take the family for a swim, or go for an after-dinner walk.

Monday the 12th. This should be a good day to take care of routine health matters. Consider seeing the dentist or doctor for a check-up. Make healthy eating easier by stopping at the produce store to stock up on good fruits and vegetables. A pet project can provide you with a focus for your industrious mind this evening.

Tuesday the 13th. People seem to be quite social now, so take time to chat with co-workers around the water cooler. Relationships should prove to be quite romantic and harmonious at this time. First dates will go well and are quite likely to turn into second dates. Beautify your domestic surroundings by bringing home fresh-cut flowers after work.

Weekly Summary

Time spent away from the spotlight can be good for your soul at present. Reflection can help you to get in touch with your heart's desires and true emotional needs. They may have been covered up by the business of life this past few weeks. Go down to the seashore, or retreat into the mountains. Nature's serenity can do much to help you to regain your own.

You may want to do things more independently than usual at this time. Try to take the feelings of a partner into consideration at the same time, however. Give reassurance of your devotion. Pursue projects at work that allow you to work on your own or that require you to get out of the office for a little while.

Browsing through antique stores or flea markets can be a good way for you to make some extra cash right now, if you are willing to put in a little work. You can find hidden treasures at this time that can bring in quite a tidy profit with a little refurbishing. You may be able to become your own boss this way.

20th Week/May 14–20

Wednesday the 14th. There may be a high level of buzz around you; expect news to be coming in. You may be attending a seminar of some type, or be involved in a meeting to bounce ideas off each other. A money idea will pay off in the long run. Pass it by a savvy friend to get more input.

Thursday the 15th. This will be one of the more intense days of the month for you. Lie low, and don't push the envelope now. Physically you need more rest, so avoid driving yourself too hard. The people around you are emotional and reactive at this time, so tread carefully with colleagues and sensitive family members.

Friday the 16th. Domestic concerns may be a significant part of the scenario. You and a partner may disagree on something, but you should also be able to come to a suitable compromise through discussion. Avoid being paranoid around a particular co-worker at this time. Realize that although she or he may exhibit jealous tendencies, they tend to be relatively harmless.

Saturday the 17th. Your good humor and enjoyment of life should draw people to you. Laughter can be the best medicine, and you can be doing a lot of it right now. Avoid coming across as too blunt in your speech, however. A road trip may be on the agenda. This can also be a good time to take a more extended vacation.

Sunday the 18th. Your love life can be quite interesting now. If you are single, someone new and unusual is likely to enter it. This person can be a fellow adventurer, as well as being pretty intelligent. The travel industry can be lucky for you right now. You may be offered a job as a travel writer or travel consultant.

Monday the 19th. You probably are in a serious frame of mind. Arrive at work early this morning, and get down to business. Expect to be commended on your high level of efficiency and productivity. Do not view a setback on a project as the end of the world. In fact, it may be a blessing in disguise.

Tuesday the 20th. You may find yourself in high demand. A phone call from a headhunter can put you in top contention for a high-level job. Consider taking on the challenge. A younger person may call you teacher and come to you for some expert advice at this time. Avoid preaching, but share your many experiences instead.

Weekly Summary

This can be a good week to invest in home renovation, redecoration, or landscaping. The time and money that you put into it now will not only add to the financial value of your home, but to your enjoyment of it as well. Consider consulting professionals for advice, as they can save you a lot of time and money in the long run.

Your creative side seems to be feeling neglected at this time. Allow it to come out. Sit down with the kids and do some finger painting. Instead of reading stories to them, make some up yourself. You may find that you have quite a talent for it, even if it does take a little more effort.

Having a regular fitness and diet routine can be your key to health right now. Join a yoga or a martial arts class with a friend. That way, you are less prone to cancel out at the last minute. Taking a healthy cooking class can be another creative and empowering way to incorporate healthy eating into your life.

21st Week/May 21–27

Wednesday the 21st. Mix-ups in communications may be significant, so check all appointment times before leaving home. Leave earlier than planned when traveling; planes may be delayed and traffic may be snarled. Make hard-and-fast appointments if you want to avoid disappointment. Try to be flexible and just go with the flow right now.

Thursday the 22nd. You and a partner may not see eye to eye on a significant issue. Resolving the matter may take some ingenuity, but you can come to some sort of win-win solution if you work together now. A close friend from the past may make an unexpected appearance this evening. You will reconnect as if no time had passed at all.

Friday the 23rd. You may acquire some money. Some of you will receive a bonus or commission from work. A tax rebate can yield more than you had thought, or maybe a lottery ticket pays off. This can be a good time to work out a strategy for your future economic security. Look over your existing portfolio. A professional may have some profitable advice for you now.

Saturday the 24th. You will appreciate some quiet time now. Take the phone off the hook, or go for a tramp in the woods. Your compassionate nature may get the best of you when a stray animal follows you home at this time. Attempt to find its owner, but you probably will be secretly thrilled if no one shows up.

Sunday the 25th. Travel and adventure may be what excite you this Sunday. If you cannot get away for a trip right away, plan one for when you can. Physical exercise may be beneficial to your mental and emotional well-being right now. Join an enthusiastic friend and do something active together this afternoon. This evening may best be spent playing games with the kids.

Monday the 26th. Keep a tight grip on your checkbook. You are more prone than usual to impulse-buying. Take a list when you go grocery shopping, or your bill can jump considerably. You love to initiate projects now, but following through to completion may be difficult. You do best as an overseer of others at this time.

Tuesday the 27th. An international deal may have you negotiating with people from afar. If you're lucky, you will get to visit with them face-to-face. Also, if you are lucky, you will be the recipient of a love letter in the mail. It may be from a secret admirer, or perhaps from a current love interest. It should definitely put a smile on your face.

Weekly Summary

Although you may usually like to run things, you may let others take the lead this week. This can be an auspicious time for you to sit back and let others perform. If you are always the one in charge, you may never get to see how well others can do under pressure. This can apply to your spouse as well. Let others make the decisions for a change.

You may now be wanting to learn more about the mysteries of life. Some of you may visit astrologers for readings, or take up the study yourselves. You can attract a very wise person to your life right now. This person may never give advice, but you can take him or her on as your guru of some sort.

A trip abroad can offer you the excitement of a lifetime right now. You may be feeling this energy inside you, urging you to get away for a while. Listen to it. Staying focused on work is difficult, so you might as well take the time off.

22nd Week/May 28–June 3

Wednesday the 28th. You have the capacity now to stay focused on one thing until it is completed. You tend to be disciplined, so set your goals high. The little luxuries in life may appeal to you more than usual, so treat yourself to a massage or facial this afternoon. Think of it as a reward for all your hard work.

Thursday the 29th. You can find yourself working in close contact with bigwigs. Your natural charisma and magnetism should serve you well in such interaction, so expect to make a dynamite impression. A job offer of some sort may come out of it all. A financial opportunity may need to be investigated further before you feel confident about investing in it.

Friday the 30th. This can be an incredibly auspicious day for new beginnings, especially in the areas of romance and communications. Someone you first lay eyes on now may turn out to be very important to your romantic future. Follow your instincts in this regard. This can be a good time to take off on a trip or to start a new course of study.

Saturday the 31st. You will be out and around a fair bit. There seems to be a buzz in the air right now, and people are quite energetic. Avoid becoming mentally hyperactive yourself. Ground yourself through physical work or exercise. Too much mental activity can be wearing right now. Nourish your physical body with hearty food this evening.

Sunday June 1st. Have a low-key morning, and then join some friends for brunch later on. Browse bookstores this afternoon. Pick up the latest bestseller, or get your hands on that classical novel that you have always promised yourself that you would read one day. You can absorb information quite quickly now, so reading and writing should be a breeze.

Monday the 2nd. Security may be very important to you at the moment. You may want to deal only with people whom you trust, and you may feel vulnerable around those whom you don't. This can be a good time to tend to the home fires. Cozy up your nest. Bake some bread or some cookies to add that wonderful and familiar smell to your environment.

Tuesday the 3rd. Your intuition should be dead-on target, so feel free to trust it. Your ability to tune in to the feelings of others now may even be considered psychic. But do not burden yourself with the problems of the rest of the world. This can be a good time to meditate on a problem, to indulge in fantasy storytelling or reading, or to be romantic with a loved one.

Weekly Summary

A new job offer can have you thinking about your future this week. This new job may encompass a whole new field of endeavor, possibly in an area in which you have limited experience. Consider taking the challenge on. At the very least you can learn a lot more about yourself and your abilities. You may even uncover a new interest or latent talent.

Being part of a group can be important to your self-esteem right now. Making a worthwhile contribution at the same time may be even more vital. Consider joining a local civil action group of some sort. You can be an incredible leader if you have passion for a cause. You can also be a wonderful supporter or rally leader for a political cause or candidate.

Taking some time out of your busy schedule for rest and relaxation is very important to prevent burnout right now. Even an hour or two every day can make a big difference, as long as you are consistent in it. Go to a restful lake or a mountain cabin to commune with nature.

23rd Week/June 4–10

Wednesday the 4th. The world can be your oyster now, so get out there and enjoy it. This should be a good time to ask directly for what you want, as people will help you to get it. Remember what they say about being careful what you ask for, however. Your optimistic mood may be contagious, and you can inspire others with your confidence.

Thursday the 5th. Your animal magnetism can be at a peak. Don't be surprised if you get approached more than once right now. If you are single, you can afford to take your pick of dates. One person in particular may impress you with his or her intelligent wit. This can be a good time to go shopping for clothes that make you look and feel good.

Friday the 6th. You may be required to prove what you know at work. Your apparent confidence should make your obvious expertise even more impressive to those watching. Avoid coming across as too bossy with a younger friend, who may not have as much life experience as you do. Allow people to make and learn from their own mistakes.

Saturday the 7th. A decision you made last Saturday may be falling short of expectations at this time. Don't despair. It is still a good decision, but it may just need some fine-tuning. A financial matter should be taken care of right away, if only to set your mind to rest. Pay bills and balance the household budget.

Sunday the 8th. You seem to be quite a stickler for details just now. Avoid coming across as a perfectionist, however. If a spouse asks for your opinion on something, avoid being critical. All your loved one may be asking for is your support. Healthy living can be quite important to you right now. Stock up on your vitamin supply.

Monday the 9th. Avoid getting involved in a power play at work this morning. A colleague may try to recruit you into siding with him on some important issue. Stay neutral, as you will not come out looking good if you get involved right now. A female you meet now may have some information important to your future. Listen up.

Tuesday the 10th. You may be feeling slightly irritated this morning, but this feeling should pass as the day wears on. Avoid arguing over the little things. This can be a good time to get a haircut or to buy dress-up clothing. Plan on doing something special for your mate this evening, as the timing appears to be conducive to romance.

Weekly Summary

You may be thinking about a new look for your personal image or style this week. It can be a very good time to buy clothes that reflect the real you. A stylish haircut will be met with approval from someone special. Add a little color to your wardrobe. Attracting attention can work well for you at this time.

A financial issue may need to be dealt with once and for all. You may have been avoiding it because of money constraints. Sit down with a practical friend or a professional and make a plan. Once a suitable strategy is in place, you can relax knowing that things are being taken care of.

Keeping yourself socially up to date can be important to you right now. You may be on everyone's social list, and you should be kept very busy with dinners and parties and gallery openings. You are a favorite guest, as your poise and elegance are likely to add grace to every gathering. Consider throwing a shindig yourself right now, as it should be quite successful.

24th Week/June 11–17

Wednesday the 11th. You may want to stick close to home and tend to domestic matters. A family member may need some special attention. This can be a good time to invest in real estate or property holdings. Those of you looking to rent an apartment or find a roommate should have good luck right about now.

Thursday the 12th. Your love life may heat up now. Someone whom you meet purely by chance can find you just as attractive as you find him or her. Be aware that this romance could burn out just as quickly as it begins, however. Avoid getting involved in a get-rich-quick scheme, even if it comes to you through a trusted friend.

Friday the 13th. In your personal life, you may be the center of attention. Several admirers can make themselves known to you now. If you are already partnered, expect to be catered to now a little more than usual. All this attention can go to a person's head though, so stay appreciative and humble. Go out and kick up your heels this evening.

Saturday the 14th. Those around you will be more emotionally intense than usual this weekend. You may be feeling rather sensitive yourself. Avoid taking something a colleague says too personally. Information may come to light allowing you to have a revelation or two about an important relationship. All the pieces of the puzzle may finally be at hand.

Sunday the 15th. You may need to keep busy now in order to be happy. If you are feeling really ambitious, this can be a good time to take care of major home repairs or yard work. Setting yourself a goal for the day can be a good way to ensure self-satisfaction when it is reached. A family member may need some extra support this evening.

Monday the 16th. You are taking career concerns very seriously these days. This can be a good time to submit resumes or to go for interviews, as you should project a very favorable and professional image. Some of you will receive a promotion or a raise in salary. Allow yourself time to have a personal life, however.

Tuesday the 17th. Your negotiating skills can be enhanced. You can successfully compromise with a colleague in order to get a project done on time. Group activities promise to be good for you at this time. Hanging around other successful and motivated people can help to keep you inspired as well. Spend time with a close friend tonight.

Weekly Summary

You may be given the green light financially to buy a house or piece of property this week. This can also be a very auspicious time to consider renovating the home that you already have. Those of you who are looking to move or to find a new roommate should be successful. Word of mouth may yield the best results, however. Ask around.

Since June is a month for celebrations, you probably will be invited to more social affairs. Expect to find yourself attending weddings, graduations, or class or family reunions at this time. Start going shopping for party clothes at once. This way you can alleviate the pressure of looking for that perfect outfit at the last minute.

You may find that the details of projects take longer to wrap up than you had anticipated. You can be spending more time at your desk right now than you usually do, trying to finalize things. Double-check the work of all other employees or contributors. There may be some minor mistakes that get overlooked if you are not careful.

25th Week/June 18–24

Wednesday the 18th. You may be thrust into the position of defending your ideas. Those who oppose you will want to see all the facts. Be ready. It may be in your best interest to allow a partner to take the lead in making some social plans right now. Just sit back and trust in the outcome. You should be delighted.

Thursday the 19th. Your personal magnetism is enhanced. You can successfully approach other people with requests or favors at this time. Those of you who are looking for investors may find what you need now. A flirtation can go a step further, if you want it to. Escape the world this evening by going to the cinema or reading a really riveting novel.

Friday the 20th. You probably are viewing the world through rose-colored glasses at the moment. Avoid giving business contacts the benefit of the doubt without reviewing all the pertinent information first. This can be a wonderful time for romance. Spend some quality time with a love interest this evening. Make sure candlelight and music are involved too. Creative types can find the inspiration that they need now.

Saturday the 21st. You can blend creative aspirations with practical focus and discipline. This should be prime productive time for writers, artists, and others who use imagination in their work. Some of you may come into some unexpected money now. An insurance policy may pay off, or a friend may repay a long overdue debt. It had slipped your mind, but you will be glad to have the cash.

Sunday the 22nd. Your energy level may be quite high, so try to find a constructive outlet for it. You can achieve an incredible amount now if you apply yourself to something specific. Travel may be on the agenda at this time. Go someplace exciting and new. Adventure travel may be something that you find gives you the thrill that you have been craving.

Monday the 23rd. You may see things with a broader perspective than usual. This can work to your advantage when dealing with promotional or advertising campaigns. Your love life may be very intense right now. Do something active or athletic together to transmute the energy in a positive manner. Try waterskiing, biking, or hiking.

Tuesday the 24th. You will want to forge ahead with career plans and project ideas, but you may come across some resistance. This may be from the boss, a partner, or even your own doubts. As long as you can show that you have done your homework, other people are likely to support you instead of opposing you.

Weekly Summary

You may be considering taking a giant step forward in your primary relationship this week. This can mean commitment, or it can mean marriage. This is not the time to act impulsively. Realize that there is no real reason to be in any rush. Be sure to talk over things with your partner, and together you should know what kind of timing is best for both of you.

This can be a good time to review all your insurance policies and warranties. Changes that you make in the amount of your coverage can better reflect your current financial situation. If you don't have any insurance, you should consider getting some right now.

Check whether your computer or appliances are still covered under warranty.

Taking a little trip now may be just what you need to add some excitement to your life. Join a friend on a vacation to a sunny locale. Although it may seem impulsive and spontaneous, you will be very glad that you went. If you are single, expect to make a love connection along the way.

26th Week/June 25–July 1

Wednesday the 25th. You may become involved in office politics now. Avoid coming across as inflexible with higher-ups and colleagues. State your point of view, but in a way that is neither blaming nor judgmental to ensure that you get heard. A profitable investment opportunity can come your way via a female friend or relative at this time.

Thursday the 26th. This can be a very auspicious time to go shopping, as you should be able to find some amazing bargains. Look for good deals on designer clothing, as it allows you to project a winning and stylish image. This can also be a very good time to invest in art or precious gemstones and jewelry.

Friday the 27th. You realize that your communicative skills are enhanced. Elect to give verbal presentations to clients or to colleagues now. You can win people over at this time and help them to see your point of view. Although you enjoy keeping busy now, avoid scattering your energies. Focus in on one or two major projects to ensure successful completion.

Saturday the 28th. Your social life will be active. Expect to receive more phone calls than usual from friends and prospective dates. If you are single, someone intelligent and charming may come into your life. A meeting of the minds may ensue and draw you in. Spend time with friends this evening. Go to a party, or throw one yourself.

Sunday the 29th. Whatever you begin today will work out to your advantage within the coming month. This can be an auspicious time to begin projects that involve your domestic life. Start a home renovation project, or begin to redecorate the living room. Consider getting the extended family together for a reunion. If not now, start to plan it for later in the summer.

Monday the 30th. You may be inclined to stick close to home. Try to arrange working from there if at all possible. You seem to enjoy domestic pursuits these days. Try out a new recipe in the kitchen, or rearrange the furniture in the living room to get a new look. A family member may have a surprising revelation this evening.

Tuesday, July the 1st. Your dry sense of humor can lift the more serious spirits of those around you. You bring light and life into any room that you happen to walk into now. A mate may want to have a serious discussion about the relationship this evening. Hear your love out completely and supportively. You should end up being closer than ever.

Weekly Summary

Thinking of a complete change of career? You may feel that you need something more challenging or exciting. Instead of completely starting over, consider taking on new and different responsibilities within your current situation. You feel that you need to be a leader of some sort, so aim high. Talk to the boss, or start something on your own.

You may find yourself wanting to participate in more group situations right now. Even joining a health club can make working out more fun. Consider taking a yoga class, or attend drop-in recreational badminton or volleyball games. Your social circle can expand as a result of any group that you join at this time.

You may be wanting to shun the limelight for a while right now. Take time to lie low and to recharge your batteries. You can utilize this time to plan your next move in a professional or personal situation. Protect your privacy by taking off to a secluded locale for a day or two. A trusted friend or loved one may be a good companion.

27th Week/July 2–8

Wednesday the 2nd. Things are now going your way. Express your ideas or thoughts to others now, and they are likely to get approved and supported. This should be a good time to ask important people important favors. You can successfully resolve a minor conflict with a friend or family member more easily now. Challenge a friend to a game of tennis this evening.

Thursday the 3rd. It may be time to renegotiate an alliance, with either a friend or a business associate. It may be that the person no longer has your best interests at heart. Ease out of the association in order to allow someone more loyal into your life. You seem to come across larger than life right now. Bowl over a date this evening.

Friday the 4th. You are mentally on the ball this Independence Day. If you are networking, you may have the chance to nab a new client or make a competitive offer when on the job. It can be your quick action that allows you to win out over other players. A concert and fireworks can end a busy day.

Saturday the 5th. You can find yourself in communication with a wide variety of people. Don't be surprised if you are on the phone, sending e-mail, or doing a lot of writing right now. You might want to be more disciplined with your health habits now. Start a new dietary or exercise program with the help of someone who is an expert.

Sunday the 6th. If you have been waiting to hear some news, expect it to come in now. There is likely to be a high level buzz around you, even if it is your day off. Friends may want to interact socially with you at this time, and you may receive an invitation to brunch. Your love life can improve dramatically.

Monday the 7th. You may hit a minor snag in a love or business relationship. An issue comes up that causes you to see the other person in a different light. Refrain from judgment, however. Negotiation and compromise can resolve things at this time. A recent decision may look less intelligent in retrospect.

Tuesday the 8th. Having a stable and loving home and love life will be much more important than usual to you. Some of you may get engaged, and some of you will decide to invest in real estate. Either way, you can successfully create stability for yourself at this time. Something you feared was lost may turn up someplace low and dark.

Weekly Summary

You are more likely than usual to put plans into action at this time. Stop thinking so much about what you want to accomplish. Just do it. You may be supported in your independence. Possibly you have been waiting a long time for the right moment to arrive, and this may very well be it. Put your doubts aside, and have confidence in yourself.

You can make some smart financial moves this week. Don't keep putting your money into something that may be draining you emotionally. If the situation is too risky or worrisome for you, get out now. Find something more stable and conservative to invest in. You can still make a sizable profit in the long run, and feel calm and confident about it as well.

You have the gift of clarity and foresight in your thinking at this time. Making important decisions is much easier now, as you can see the bigger picture. This can be a good time to set up the monthly budget, or to decide what kind of new car to buy.

28th Week/July 9–15

Wednesday the 9th. You will want to be in control of things now. Try to let go; trust in the abilities of those around you. A love interest may be coming across as too demanding at this time. Perhaps it is caused by insecurity. Reassure the individual of your intentions and affection. Spend time with family this evening.

Thursday the 10th. You can expect to be in a cheerful and optimistic mood. A friend will grant you a favor when asked, but you may need to break through some resistance first. An old friend from the past may make a surprise appearance now. This can be a good time to resolve and forgive an old issue from the past.

Friday the 11th. Your charm and magnetism are at a peak. Romance is in the air, and you may be at the top of a few people's date list. Keep things lighthearted now; this is not the time to discuss anything serious. Take advantage of all this romantic atmosphere and dash out to a party this evening.

Saturday the 12th. Outdoor adventure can be what motivates you this weekend. Join a friend or a loved one for a long hike or bike ride. You are a great event organizer yourself right now, so consider getting people together for a rafting trip or a lakeside picnic. Someone whom you meet from another country may end up becoming a good friend.

Sunday the 13th. Your work ethic may be in high gear. Even if you have the day off, you still may want to be productive. Working in the earth should bring satisfaction now. Dig around in the garden, or start landscaping the yard. Family members or in-laws may drop in unexpectedly, so make sure the larder is full.

Monday the 14th. Expect your love life to be more unpredictable or volatile than usual. If you are single, a coincidental meeting with an acquaintance can turn into something more romantic. The attraction is likely to be sudden and mutual. If already partnered, this is a good time to add some spice to your life by trying some new and exciting things together.

Tuesday the 15th. You may find yourself in the spotlight for your work efforts. You can receive kudos from the boss for a job well done. A promotion or a raise may be part of the package as well. To avoid being disappointed, do not put someone that you admire up on a pedestal. Remember such people are only human too.

Weekly Summary

You may find yourself taking on more responsibilities and commitments at this time, especially in your personal and domestic life. You can be feeling slightly overwhelmed with it all. Don't worry. You rise to the occasion beautifully, and things should fall into place. A partner or family member might be a big support for you right now.

Your creativity can make you some money if you want it to. You may not realize your own talent. A hobby that you love can turn out to be quite lucrative. Ask for the advice of a savvy business friend on how to go about doing this. Once you hear what your friend has to say, you will become excited and motivated to proceed.

This can be a good time to pay attention to health, diet, and exercise. You should be able to kick any bad habits more easily than usual at this time, as your motivation and discipline are high. Consider consulting a nutritionist to help make up a plan with the least amount of hassle.

29th Week/July 16–22

Wednesday the 16th. You may feel like you are on a roller coaster where your love life is concerned. If a relationship breaks up at this time, realize that this can make room for the right person to enter your life. If you are with the right one already, deal with a minor conflict now before it escalates into something bigger.

Thursday the 17th. The people around you are in a compassionate mood now. The bank may be more likely to grant you a loan, or a friend more likely to grant you a favor. Money may come to you unexpectedly when a friend repays a debt from long ago. Some of you may be winners of lottery prizes at this time.

Friday the 18th. Watch your speech. You probably come across as blunt or impatient at this time, and more sensitive types may take your words to heart. Your head and your heart are in agreement about a financial or business idea. Do your homework first before making any financial decisions, however. Enjoy a movie and some popcorn this evening.

Saturday the 19th. You may be taking off for an extended vacation. If not, try to get away for a short one instead. Take a road trip to the nearest beach or lake and unwind with a close friend. Your love life may hit a bumpy patch in the road this evening, but things should eventually smooth out once again.

Sunday the 20th. You may be asked to partake in some kind of religious or spiritual ritual. Accepting the invitation will mean a lot to someone special. You are quite bossy and impatient right now. Channel your energies into projects where you can be the leader. Physical endeavors are favored now, so get outdoors for some exercise.

Monday the 21st. You may feel as if no one can stop you now, and probably nobody can. You may have made up your mind about a situation and are not letting anybody else's opinion sway you. Good for you for staying focused and committed to your cause. You may even inspire others to jump onto your bandwagon, now.

Tuesday the 22nd. You seem to be quite committed and productive on the work front. Avoid coming across as inflexible with a co-worker or employee right now, however. Realize that your way may not be the only way. The little luxuries in life are important to you now. Treat yourself to something new or something decadent this afternoon.

Weekly Summary

A new business venture is probably going to get the green light this week. You should be able to get it off the ground with the right backer. Get the word out to as many people as you can, and someone should come forward quite quickly. A relative may show some interest, but be careful. You can afford to be choosy about whom you want to be partners with now.

Consider taking some courses to expand your knowledge in a particular aspect of your career. This can be a very smart move on your part, putting you ahead of the competition. Although it may take longer to achieve your goal in some respects, it can ensure your success when you do eventually make your move.

You may find yourself in the spotlight in some way right now. You can be the recipient of an honor at work or in connection with your career. Pay no attention to the jealous mutterings of resentful colleagues. They should eventually come around to wish you well.

30th Week/July 23–29

Wednesday the 23rd. You will be kept busy running errands. If you have been waiting for some news, you may receive it now. A sibling or relative may be trying to dump a family responsibility onto your shoulders.

Compromise, and you can find an equitable solution for everyone concerned. Attend a book signing or reading this evening.

Thursday the 24th. If you are in the market for new electronic equipment, this can be the day to purchase some. Look for bargains in computers, cell phones, or stereo components. Do your research first, so you can get the best price from the salesperson, however. A younger male friend may need your input on a personal problem this evening. Lend an ear.

Friday the 25th. You come across as quite witty and communicative just now. This should be a very auspicious time to start a new class of some sort, as you seem to retain information well these days. You may have a good ear for languages and for accents. Share your creative ideas with those who can appreciate them.

Saturday the 26th. Stay close to home this morning and take care of domestic chores and tasks. Get the whole household involved, and delegate responsibilities to each person. You should finish things up in no time. This can be a great day for a picnic with the extended family. Don't be surprised if everyone goes all out with the food preparation.

Sunday the 27th. This will be a good time to tend to domestic affairs. If you have been wanting to redecorate the house, start doing it now. You lean toward items that lend warmth and coziness to a room. You do not have to spend a lot. A bit of paint and a few yards of fabric can make a world of difference.

Monday the 28th. Whatever you begin now will achieve its goals within a month. This should be a good time to put creative work out on the market, or to submit projects for approval. You really shine brightly right now, so don't let this auspicious time go to waste. You can successfully begin self-improvement projects at this time as well.

Tuesday the 29th. Be direct; ask for what you want, and people may make room for you now. This should be a good time to ask important people for their backing, or to ask the landlord for an extension on the rent. Your love life will be more exciting than usual right now. If you are single, you may meet someone through a friend this evening.

Weekly Summary

This can be a good time to allow your creative side more freedom in your life. You may have some untapped talent in the area of music or art. If you have ever wanted to learn a new instrument, now is the perfect time to sign up for some lessons. Some of you may be interested in a more physical pursuit, such as dance.

It may be time to think about investing in a new vehicle, especially if there are teenagers in the house. Technically, a new car will save you time and money in the long run, especially if repair bills are starting to come in on your existing car. Check consumer magazines or on-line forums to get some ballpark figures.

You can still redecorate the house at this time even if you are on a tight budget. Although your tastes may be classic and expensive, you can find some great deals at garage sales. You may just need to do a little refinishing. Adding a new color paint to the walls can change the entire feel of a room.

31st Week/July 30–August 5

Wednesday the 30th. Your money-management skills may be put to the test now. This is an auspicious time to go over the budget and to see where you can cut some corners with the least amount of sacrifice. A little bit here and there can add up to a lot over the long term. A younger relative may have some surprising, but pleasant, news tonight.

Thursday the 31st. You will be efficient and productive on the job at the moment. This can be a good time to clean up the details of old and incomplete projects before moving ahead with new ones. A female friend may ask you to do something that you have reservations about. Trust your intuition on this one, and be responsible to your own needs and wants.

Friday August 1st. Your level of physical energy should be quite high. Find a constructive outlet for it through exercise or manual labor. If you don't, your energy may come out as irritation with the people around you. An important male in your life may be more demanding or bossy than usual now. Stand your ground.

Saturday the 2nd. You will appreciate beauty and harmony in your surroundings this weekend. Spend time in places that appeal to your fine sensibilities right now. Browse the art gallery, or visit the museum. Spend time beautifying yourself as well. Schedule a facial or a manicure this afternoon, and then dress up for an evening on the town tonight.

Sunday the 3rd. You may see the world as you want to see it, rather than as it actually is. Enjoy your romantic visions now, and leave the everyday chores and tasks for another time. This can be a good day for the movies or for an afternoon of live theater. Avoid making any important decisions until you are in a more realistic frame of mind.

Monday the 4th. You should rethink a decision made a while back. Recent developments may have changed the whole picture; start revision at this time. More information can now be available. Make the necessary adjustments and continue on. You can profit from the buying or selling of real estate. Those of you who are looking for a new place to rent should have success now.

Tuesday the 5th. You exude charm and magnetism now. If you are single, expect to be approached by more than one admirer. You can afford to be choosy at this time. Impress the boss and win big points by inviting him over for dinner this evening. Polish the silver and bring out the best china and linens.

Weekly Summary

Spending time nurturing others will be very satisfying to you this week. If you have kids, you probably will be spending a lot of time with them. If you don't, there may be other ways to fulfill this need. Nurture plants and flowers instead. You can get a lot out of visiting an elderly relative or friend at this time.

Your communication skills are enhanced this week. You may be thrust into the position of having to be extra alert during a routine meeting at work. Be ready with the facts in case you are called upon to give an impromptu presentation. You can win over clients and opponents alike.

Those of you who are in the market for a new home probably will be successful at this time. While house hunting, you may come across one that is perfect, but out of your price range. Make an offer anyway. It may just be accepted. It should result in a profitable deal for you.

32nd Week/August 6–12

Wednesday the 6th. You may be viewing the world through rose-colored glasses now. Avoid putting love interests up on a pedestal. Be realistic; remember that they are human too. Travel may look good to you, but you may not be able to shake loose enough time for the trip of your dreams. So become an armchair traveler instead.

Thursday the 7th. It may be more difficult than usual for you to stay pinned to one location. Work on projects that allow you to move around a fair bit. An international deal can be in the making now, and it is likely to be a very successful and profitable negotiation. This should be an auspicious time to start classes or to take exams.

Friday the 8th. Stay flexible; things may not go now according to plan. Your primary relationship may be put on the back burner because of priorities in other areas. Be sure to explain these priorities in detail to your beloved to avoid hurt feelings. You can bring interesting ideas to the table when interacting with colleagues this afternoon.

Saturday the 9th. You feel very powerful now and should be able to accomplish anything that you set your mind to. It may take longer than anticipated, however, but persevere. You may be on the receiving end of some privileged information that can help your financial or business life right now. Keep it under your hat for a while.

Sunday the 10th. You probably find yourself interacting with a wide variety of people. A private brunch date with a friend can turn out to be more like a party when others join you. Accept the situation and just enjoy the camaraderie. You and your friend can chat another time. Avoid coming across as too detached in relation to a child this evening.

Monday the 11th. Your emotions may run higher than usual. Expect those around you to be more emotionally volatile right now as well. This may not be the best day for confrontations or negotiations. Wait until everyone has more time to calm down and be in a better frame of mind. Your love life may respond favorably to these intense vibrations and should be all you may desire.

Tuesday the 12th. If you stay focused, you should get much accomplished. It may be easier to daydream now, however. Consider combining the two by focusing in on some kind of creative activity or project. This should be a good time to think up advertising slogans or to write reports or stories that capture the imagination of the listeners. Use humor to good advantage now.

Weekly Summary

Setting a positive example for your children can make a huge difference to them at this time. They may want to spend some quality time with you right now. Consider getting involved in charity or volunteer work with them. Take the whole family to the local animal shelter and do some dog-walking. The kids will love it.

Your social life is about to pick up tremendously at this time. Expect to receive invitations to graduations, weddings, reunions, and parties. Your social calendar is bound to be packed now, but you will enjoy this time enormously. If you cannot fit everything in, you can afford to be choosy as to which invitations to accept right now.

You may be attracted to a much younger individual at this time. Don't let onlookers judge you in this matter, as age should not make a difference to the heart. This relationship can turn out to be quite special, and this person can help you to stay light and bright. Even if this is purely a platonic friendship, you both will benefit from it a great deal.

33rd Week/August 13–19

Wednesday the 13th. You may be called upon to defend your position. A financial or investment opportunity presented to you now may not be what you are looking for at this time. Don't let consideration for a friend's feelings sway your good judgment in this matter. An in-depth discussion with a mate this evening should help to restore or enhance domestic harmony.

Thursday the 14th. You probably will receive some unexpected financial benefits, which can be in the form of an insurance payment, a commission, or a winning lottery ticket. Take some of it and treat yourself to something special. Pay attention to your dreams this evening. They may hold the answer to a problem that you have been wondering about lately.

Friday the 15th. This should be a very auspicious day as far as love and money are concerned. If you are single, expect someone attractive to pay attention to you now. First dates will go well, as will romantic evenings with the one you love. You can profit from investments made in products that promote health and beauty at this time.

Saturday the 16th. You seem to get along well with just about everyone now. You can make a good impression wherever you go. This should be a good time to go for job interviews or auditions. If a party is not on your calendar, throw one yourself. Don't miss this great opportunity to socialize and to have fun now. An important contact can be made this evening.

Sunday the 17th. You may want to have a low-key day. Catch up on your sleep, and then meet a friend for brunch or a leisurely stroll through the park. You appreciate life through your senses right now, so schedule a massage. Good food may be especially important, so take time to prepare a sumptuous dinner for this evening.

Monday the 18th. You may be fielding offers for a new job, but don't let a sense of urgency cause you to take something you don't really want. Do your groundwork, and the perfect thing is likely to make itself known to you very soon. A setback at home can turn out to be a blessing in disguise. Spend some quality time with the family tonight.

Tuesday the 19th. This seems to be a good time to organize and clear out your home or office. Throw out things that you no longer need. Send some old clothes to a consignment store, or donate them to charity. Clearing things out this way can symbolically make room for new things to enter your life. You will feel less chaotic as a result.

Weekly Summary

This can be an auspicious time to invest in property or real estate. If you are looking to rent a home, you have a good chance of finding something that you really like at this time. The key may be to be clear on exactly what it is that you want. Be sure that both you and your partner are in agreement on this. Once you have done that, the right place can magically appear.

The travel bug may be hitting you harder than usual right now. A change of scenery may be just what you need. Consider using your vacation time to venture forth on a trip. If no one seems to be available to accompany you at this time, go on your own. The fresh perspective you receive as a result should make a world of difference.

You may be rebelling against authority even more than usual this week. Some of you may be considering going out on your own and starting up your own business. This should be an auspicious time to do so. You do best when working independently or as the boss. Seek out a close friend who can provide astute advice in this area.

34th Week/August 20–26

Wednesday the 20th. Lady Luck is on your side as far as love and money are concerned. Financial speculation works in your favor now, but only if you are moderately conservative. Variety may be the spice of life at this time. Socialize with different people this evening. Your world may open up in new ways as a result.

Thursday the 21st. This can be a great day for communications and negotiations. Purchase new computers, stereos, cell phones, and even cars right now. It also is a very auspicious day to open the doors of a new business or to start any kind of new project. Submit manuscripts to publishers, or set off on a long trip.

Friday the 22nd. Expect the unexpected today. If you are single, you may come into contact with someone very attractive, but who may be quite unlike your usual type. Go with it, as you can end up widening your romantic horizons as a result. A get-rich-quick scheme may not deliver what it promises at this time. Pass on the offer to get involved.

Saturday the 23rd. This is a good time to catch up on some rest and relaxation. Put all business aside for now and take off for some place quiet and idyllic. A seaside resort or mountain retreat with a loved one or trusted friend can be just the thing. Even a quiet afternoon at home reading a book can help to recharge tired batteries.

Sunday the 24th. Domestic pursuits can provide more satisfaction than usual. Try out that new recipe on the family, or get started on some early canning or jam making. Gardening and yard work can also provide pleasure. Roll up your sleeves and get dirty. The ground seems to be quite fertile now, so plant a few herbs or late-blooming flowers.

Monday the 25th. Things just naturally seem to go your way. This can be a good time to ask directly for what you want now. Approach the boss for a raise, or the bank for a loan. Others will also accommodate you at this time. You may need to have a talk about independence with a mate this evening.

Tuesday the 26th. You can probably charm anybody into just about anything right now. This talent should come in handy if you have to sell or negotiate deals with others. You may experience a push-pull effect in your love life this evening. What you want may not be what your partner wants, or vice versa. Compromise can work things out, however.

Weekly Summary

Don't be surprised if you need to upgrade your computer now, or want to invest in the latest in telecommunications equipment. You may find that you are fascinated by new gadgetry. This can be a good time to buy, but be sure to do your research first to avoid paying more than you have to. Consult with a friend who is well informed on technology.

You may be feeling a little overwhelmed with responsibilities this week. Be aware that you may have choices that could help to lighten your load. Your sense of duty to a loved one may be causing you to take on more than you realistically can right now. Realize that the person may be able to deal with more than you think.

You may be thinking about making a few changes in your appearance this week. Consider investing in some spiffy new clothes that will project the image that you want to the world. You may be amazed at how investing in yourself this way can perk up your confidence level. A new haircut is sure to be met with approval from someone special right now.

35th Week/August 27–September 2

Wednesday the 27th. Your temper can be pushed to the limit. You can lessen this effect by becoming less demanding or perfectionistic in your standards right now. It is possible that you are expecting too much from those around you, as well as from yourself. Relax and do your best. It should be good enough.

Thursday the 28th. You seem to be more conscious than usual of your health and dietary regimen now. A set routine can make it easier to reach your goals. Ask for the help of a professional to set up the most efficient plan. Money matters can take up your attention this afternoon. Reassess the budget, and revise it to better reflect your current needs.

Friday the 29th. Allow yourself extra time to get to and from appointments. Communications mix-ups and traffic tie-ups are inevitable. Be sure to check time schedules before you start out. Don't make appointments; people may not even show up. Your best bet may be to remain flexible and ready for whatever happens.

Saturday the 30th. You should be in a very social mood this weekend. Call up a friend whom you haven't seen for a while and make a lunch date. People are bound to be thrilled to hear from you now. A social event this evening can benefit you in more ways than one. If you are single, a romantic encounter can leave you breathless.

Sunday the 31st. Love may be on your mind. A new romantic relationship is moving ahead quite quickly at this time. If you have been seeing someone for a while, this may be the day that you become engaged. An old friend may no longer have your best interests at heart. It can be time to cut the ties.

Monday September 1st. An investment opportunity can come to your attention through friends, or relatives. Don't let their obvious enthusiasm sway your good judgment. Research the project before deciding one way or the other. A love interest is more demanding than usual at this time. There may just be some need of reassurance about where things stand right now.

Tuesday the 2nd. You probably will be active and on the go. You may be fighting a deadline that could force you to make a decision that you may not be ready to make quite yet. If you have to make it anyway, go with your gut intuition. You can trust it now. Games, sports, and outdoor activities should provide satisfaction this evening.

Weekly Summary

A co-worker may be pushing the limits of your good nature just now. Be proud of yourself for holding your temper and for employing diplomacy in the situation. There can be times when more emotional force is needed, however, and this can be one of those times. If people are not respecting you, consider letting them know it in a stronger kind of way.

Think twice before lending a large amount of money to a relative. Be clear on whether or not you can realistically expect the individual to make repayment a priority. If you are not sure, consider setting up some ground rules first to keep any future resentments from building up. It cannot hurt to get everything in writing.

A talent for craftsmanship may show itself when you are asked to submit a creative project for work or for school right now. Even you may be surprised at what you can produce when you really try. Consider honing this raw skill into something more refined by taking a course of your own. Try woodworking, sculpting, or even drawing.

36th Week/September 3–9

Wednesday the 3rd. You should be successful in any efforts made toward promotion of self or of others. You know instinctively what appeals to the masses, so this can be a good time to invest in advertising. Enjoy an activity with some friends this evening, such as water-skiing or mountain biking. Life feels good now.

Thursday the 4th. You are more likely than usual to become intensely focused on something or someone. Try to channel this intensity into a constructive outlet. Once you get going, there may be no stopping you. A love affair can become more complicated at this time. You may decide either to get more deeply involved or to let it go completely.

Friday the 5th. Things are moving along nicely now. A meeting with bigwigs this morning may exceed your highest expectations. You may emerge from it with a promotion, a raise, or a job offer. Give yourself a pat on the back. Attend a social function this evening that may be connected to your work in some way. You can gain an important ally.

Saturday the 6th. You see things as possibilities this weekend. Write down all your great ideas for future use. You may be inclined toward excess in most things right now, so try to maintain a balance in what you do. This may apply especially to physical exercise. Avoid overdoing it. Spending money impulsively can also be a temptation this weekend.

Sunday the 7th. You will enjoy being surrounded by close friends now. Someone special may express love and appreciation of you at this time. You will enjoy participating in a charity fund-raiser or community event this afternoon. Volunteer your exceptional organizational and social skills to a meaningful cause; your social circle will expand as a result.

Monday the 8th. Expect the unexpected. Keep plans flexible to accommodate any last-minute changes in your schedule. You are in a more rational and detached mood than usual right now, so avoid engaging in any deep or heartfelt discussions. Conflict resolution can go well since you see things clearly now and will not get too emotionally agitated.

Tuesday the 9th. Avoid getting involved in power struggles. Colleagues or relatives may try to manipulate you into doing what they want you to do. Don't fall for their guilt or blame game. Your intuitive abilities are enhanced at this time. Use it when advising a friend this evening. Try to remember your dreams tonight; there can be hidden messages.

Weekly Summary

This is a good time to work on your health and dietary program. If you have been wanting to get into better shape, you should be successful if you start in on a program right now. A nutritionist can help you to set up an easy and hassle-free dietary program. The time and effort saved in this way will make it that much easier to reach your goals.

You and a partner might be in conflict regarding how much time you spend together. He or she may want more of your attention. A consistent time may be what is needed to set minds at ease. As long as people know that they have a date to count on, they will let up a bit.

Take out all your insurance policies and check to

make sure that they are up to date, as well as warranties on appliances. Check your computer warranty. You may be able to get something small fixed for free if you can get in under the wire. It can be a good idea to upgrade the options on your homeowner's insurance to better reflect your current needs.

37th Week/September 10–16

Wednesday the 10th. You may feel more emotionally intense than usual. An issue between you and your mate can come to a head at this time. Try to see this as a positive event, as it should help to bring you both closer to resolution. Guard against overreacting emotionally to a business partner or a colleague this afternoon, however.

Thursday the 11th. An urge to get away from the daily grind may dominate the day. Finish work early and join a friend for some fun this afternoon. You are more inclined than usual toward taking risks right now. Athletes can break records, and drivers may have a lead foot. The in-laws may drop in unexpectedly this evening.

Friday the 12th. You probably do not have much patience for details at present. You are more of an idea person right now, so consider delegating the details for others to deal with. A rebellious attitude toward people at work may turn others off, so try to work on your own as much as possible. Freedom may be your keyword for today.

Saturday the 13th. You may be less objective than usual, and may think that your way is the right way. Avoid appearing too bossy with friends or loved ones at this time. Relax and allow others to do things in the way that works best for them. Enjoy good food, good wine, and good company this evening.

Sunday the 14th. You may seem more affectionate than usual this weekend. Although you are seen as warmhearted most of the time anyway, your generosity of spirit can soar to new heights now. You can forge a closer bond with a friend at this time, as you each can implicitly trust the loyalty of the other.

Monday the 15th. You exude extra charm these days, and others are likely to notice. If you are single, you may not be for long. An admirer can express romantic sentiments to you now. Money can be made through conservative means. Invest in long-term stocks and bonds. The beauty industry can provide another lucrative investment opportunity.

Tuesday the 16th. You seem to be in quite a social frame of mind at present. Those you work with are more than willing to take time out to chat. If you have lunch with co-workers, you can catch up on the office gossip. You may become privy to some information that can be important to your future. Spend time with a witty and fun friend this evening.

Weekly Summary

You may be experiencing an urge to break away from the routine of life right now. This is a very auspicious time to plan that trip of a lifetime. Start in on researching exactly where you want to go. The library can be a cheap, yet valuable, resource for this. Talk to people about their adventures. Personal experience is a very reliable resource sometimes.

You may be feeling that you are not being taken as seriously as you would like at work right now. This can be the perfect time to schedule a meeting with the boss, who cannot know how you feel or what you want until you put it in words. Scheduling a meeting should show that you are assertive and confident of yourself.

Being straightforward and honest in your love life may get you where you want to go right now. Let the other person know how you feel, and you may be pleasantly surprised at the results. Others appreciate honesty from you at this time, and will respect you more as a result.

38th Week/September 17–23

Wednesday the 17th. You may be asked to donate to charity. Why not donate your time instead of cash? Your wonderful organizational and leadership skills will be very much appreciated. Find a cause that has meaning for you and sign up. Important career contacts can also be made as a result. A book signing or reading may stimulate you intellectually this evening.

Thursday the 18th. This should be a good time to invest in any kind of electronic equipment. Purchase computer parts, new stereos, or cell phones. You may find that the experiences and opinions of other consumers can help you to make the right purchase. Ask around. A night school course started now should be interesting and fun.

Friday the 19th. You may be inclined to stick close to home. Putter around the house and tend to domestic chores and tasks. Baking, cooking, and canning can all provide pleasure if you are so inclined. Entertain at home this evening by throwing a dinner party. Make it a potluck so that everyone can participate by bringing their own special concoctions.

Saturday the 20th. Your energy level is high but erratic just now. Do things in short spurts in order to make the most of what time you have. Physical exercise can help, especially water sports. Get out and do some swimming or water skiing with friends or family. Be sure to allow yourself some downtime during the day to recharge your batteries, however.

Sunday the 21st. Expect the worst in communications and delays. Be sure to reconfirm all appointments before leaving home, and allow extra travel time due to the inevitable traffic snarls. Your best bet may be to just go with the flow today, and to stay flexible. Dates can be late or fail to show up at all if caught in huge traffic jams.

Monday the 22nd. Things can go your way right now, especially when you ask directly for what you want. You will be noticed and appreciated for your warmth, generosity, and charm. This should be a good time to schedule a job interview, an audition, or a verbal exam of some sort. You may need more independence than usual, however.

Tuesday the 23rd. Romance and relationships can be a big part of today's scenario. You see the beauty in all things and all people right now, which should lend itself well to romance this evening. First dates will go exceptionally well, and you may find yourself smitten right off the bat. The feeling is likely to be mutual.

Weekly Summary

Take some time for quiet reflection by going somewhere beautiful and quiet. A lakeside retreat or mountain resort would be ideal. An incredible sense of serenity and calm can help you to recharge your batteries and prepare for the new cycle starting in your life. Plan your strategy from behind the scenes now.

This should be an excellent time to get involved in a more organized kind of physical activity. The martial arts may be an activity at which you excel. Try karate, kung-fu, or even tai-chi for a more gentle discipline. Sports where competition is involved can be a good motivator as well, such as tennis or squash. Team sports may not be your best bet, however.

It may be time to revise your current budget to better reflect your needs. Try to allow a little extra for the odd indulgence now and again. This can prevent you from rebelling and blowing your budget altogether. If you know that you can treat yourself to a new item of clothing every so often, you should be more motivated to stick to your plan.

39th Week/September 24–30

Wednesday the 24th. You may be in a more serious mood than usual. A significant relationship can be going through some changes that you are not happy with. Your best bet probably will be just to go with the flow, and things should work out to your ultimate best interest. Be conservative where finances are concerned right now.

Thursday the 25th. Any projects started now should show good results within the month. This may be an especially auspicious time for new relationships, friendships, and business partnerships. Your social life may be quite active at this time. You can enjoy a cultural type of event this evening, such as a gallery opening or a wine tasting affair.

Friday the 26th. You should feel optimistic and upbeat now. You may be offered an opportunity to make money through the idea of a friend. It may have definite potential, but discuss it with someone more in the know before making any definite commitments. Get out and kick up your heels with some friends this evening. Many of you will prefer to celebrate the Rosh Hashanah holiday more quietly.

Saturday the 27th. You seem to have the gift of focus and ambition these days. This can be a good time to start on any home renovation or repair projects. Money may be an issue, so listen to the savvy advice of an older relative. A love interest may display some jealousy toward a friend of yours now. Be sure to offer reassurance of your true affections.

Sunday the 28th. Still waters run deep at present, and you may be quite content to be low-key now. This day can lend itself well to spiritual studies, journal writing, or to meditation. Your intuition should be right on target at this time. Trust it when dealing with a conflict with a friend. The individual's defensiveness may just be a cover-up for insecurity.

Monday the 29th. You should excel at self-promotion because you know just what to say to make others trust you and have confidence in your abilities. You can also promote others successfully now as well. You may be able to see the bigger picture right now, and can set your future goals accordingly.

Tuesday the 30th. You are more restless and curious than usual. You can decide to go to a planetarium or to something completely out of the ordinary. You may find yourself surrounded by new people and interested by their new and different ideas, opinions, and perspectives at this time. This can be a good time to take off on a trip.

Weekly Summary

If you have been waiting for some important news to arrive, your expectations will be rewarded. You will be pleased with what you hear. You seem to be noted for your intelligence and your wit right now. This can be a good time to entertain important people, or to make the social rounds. You are a popular and coveted guest at this time.

Love may blossom best at home this week. Invite your beloved over for a special home-cooked dinner, complete with wine and candlelight, of course. This can also be an auspicious time to invite the boss over for dinner. He or she is bound to be impressed with the effort that you make, so bring out the fine china and crystal.

You probably will be invited to some sort of special celebration. This could be a graduation or a wedding ceremony. You may have other plans at the time, but do your best to switch them. Your participation in this event can mean a lot to the invitee.

40th Week/October 1–7

Wednesday October 1st. You can find yourself interacting with someone internationally. This may be through a deal that you are in the midst of making right now. You may even get the chance to travel and to visit your contact face to face very soon. A younger family member's mistake this evening can turn out to be a blessing in disguise.

Thursday the 2nd. You may be in the throes of amending a decision that you made about one week ago. You probably did not then have all the pertinent information, but you should have it all now. Career issues are promising for you right now. An out-of-the-blue call from a headhunter may be the start of something big.

Friday the 3rd. Whatever you begin now will last a very long time. This should be an auspicious day to exchange wedding vows, to make a promise to someone, or to buy a house that you plan to live in for many years. You may need to confront a male co-worker who has no authority to throw his weight around.

Saturday the 4th. You will excel at interpersonal relationships just now. An alliance with a friend should work out to be the best interest of you both right now, especially if it involves business or finance. If you are single, you may meet the person of your dreams this evening at a social affair. Be sure to dress your best and smile a lot.

Sunday the 5th. You may be called upon to fulfill some sort of responsibility to relatives. It may be time to realize that they can take care of themselves. Try to see the situation realistically now. A mate may need to discuss something important with you this evening. Just listening is likely to be your best recourse now.

Monday the 6th. You may receive some sort of unexpected bonus, such as an insurance payment, a tax refund, or a work benefit or commission. Treat yourself to something luxurious. Some of you may spend your time in fasting and prayer for Yom Kippur. The rest of you should watch your speech, as your brand of humor may be too broad to be taken the right way by a sensitive colleague.

Tuesday the 7th. Your intuition should be right on target now. Use it to make a big financial or investment decision this morning. Make sure that you have done your homework as well, however. Your magnetism is enhanced, so your love life may move into high gear as a result. Make plans with a love interest this evening.

Weekly Summary

You are blessed with a lot of willpower right about now. Your diet and exercise goals are within reach as a result. Consider joining a health club or a fitness class to have fun and socialize while you reach your goals. A cooking class can also be a good way to learn how to cook tasty yet healthy meals.

If your love life has been fairly quiet lately, get ready for some changes. You are more charismatic and magnetic than usual, and several romantic opportunities may come your way this week. You can afford to be choosy now as well. If already partnered, expect your beloved to lavish a little extra attention on you now.

If you have been mulling over an important financial decision, avoid allowing peer pressure to influence you in any way. It may be that you need more input on the issue. Consider talking to a savvy relative or friend who has no vested interest in the project. Such an individual can bring up some important points that never occurred to you.

41st Week/October 8–14

Wednesday the 8th. You want to employ your freedom, so being tied down to one thing may be too tedious for you at this time. Work on projects that allow you some independence and movement. Any efforts made toward promotion should be met with success. A sudden and strong attraction to someone new may be exciting, but don't expect it to last.

Thursday the 9th. You probably are feeling more emotionally intense than usual. Don't be surprised to find that those around you are fairly touchy right now as well. If people close to you lose their tempers this evening, don't take it personally. Remove yourself from the situation until they calm down, and then you can talk about things more rationally.

Friday the 10th. You may feel as if there is nothing that you cannot do at present. Your sheer willpower and determination are the reason why you succeed now. An older male can be a valuable ally in a business or financial endeavor, so listen to what he has to say. You will enjoy getting away for a fun-filled weekend with friends.

Saturday the 11th. Your emotional and financial security may be uppermost in your mind now. A job change can be risky financially, but still provide you with rewards on a more personal level. If you do what you love, the money is likely to follow. Good food and good company should make for a very pleasant evening.

Sunday the 12th. You tend to be more in touch with your emotions than you usually are. They can be a valuable resource for you where a relative or close friend is concerned. But avoid taking on the problems of others. Be compassionate, yet stay detached. Spend some time with family this evening. Invite everyone over for a big dinner.

Monday the 13th. You may be seen as a chatterbox now. You seem to have lots to say, and you can say it in a way that excites and inspires others. A meeting with higher-ups should go well. You can successfully sell your idea, but make sure that you highlight the more conservative or traditional aspects of it.

Tuesday the 14th. Groups are the focus of your energy now. One work group in particular can work very well with you as the leader. If this is a union or a professional association of some kind, consider running for office. You are always happiest being the one in charge. Writers should get some plaudits for their work.

Weekly Summary

You may be thinking now of going back to school. Taking some courses to upgrade your current career skills can be a very auspicious move right now. Learning a new technique can allow you to expand into new areas within your chosen field. Some of you will simply enjoy a night school course in a field that you find fascinating.

You may be the focus at work these days, so dress for success and don't be reluctant to put in a little overtime. The boss is likely to be watching, and you can score big points. Some of you may be thrust into the spotlight by an award or honor of some sort. Remember to be humble as you receive your kudos.

Your optimism and bright disposition draw others to you right now. You can expand your social circle by volunteering your time to a charity group, or helping to organize a political rally. If you decide to get involved, an important new friendship may be the outcome.

42nd Week/October 15–21

Wednesday the 15th. Take some time for rest and relaxation. You may have been burning the candle at both ends as of late. A little downtime can make a world of difference to your perspective and to your peace of mind right now. You can defuse a potential family conflict if you act fast later in the day.

Thursday the 16th. Domestic pursuits can provide satisfaction. This can be a good time to do some baking or canning. Your reward will be the smiles on the faces of family members when they walk into a wonderful smelling kitchen. Do not purchase land or real estate until you are absolutely clear on all the details.

Friday the 17th. Let go of old things or old patterns that are no longer serving you. You can let go of a bad habit and replace it with a new one more easily than usual right now. Spend a quiet evening with a quiet friend. You both should enjoy the natural rapport that comes up between you now. Put on a CD and enjoy some classical music.

Saturday the 18th. Lady Luck is on your side. This looks like a good time to ask directly for what you want. As the saying goes, you should be careful of what you wish for however; you just may get it. A love relationship may become serious this evening. This is a good time to talk about commitment or to propose marriage.

Sunday the 19th. You may have an exaggerated need for independence now. Making plans ahead of time may feel too constricting at present, and you may want to fly by the seat of your pants. Live in the moment, and see what comes up. Be sure to explain these feelings to a partner or a loved one so that he or she does not feel left out.

Monday the 20th. This can be an auspicious time to begin any self-improvement or fitness programs. You want to look smart and make the very best impression that you can right now. Consider investing in some new clothes that reflect the real you, or the you that you want to project to the world. Treat yourself to a massage while you're at it.

Tuesday the 21st. Finances are part of the today's scenario. You probably will be successful in any endeavors to nab a new client or a new commission now. Any efforts that you make to improve your financial situation at this time will pay off. Your body may be sensitive now, so eat healthy food and stock up on your vitamins.

Weekly Summary

Take the time for some quiet reflection this week. You may not feel like being center stage at this time, and staying in the background can provide some much-needed privacy. Try to get away for a day or two to some place quiet and scenic. Communing with nature can help you to clear your head and to decide what your next move should be.

You may feel like making a change in your personal appearance. A new haircut or color will be met with approval by that someone special. You may feel like spending money on yourself right now. Shopping expeditions for clothes should be fruitful. Focus in on quality as opposed to quantity, as luxury and image appeal most to you now.

You should be able to come up with some new and creative ways to make some extra cash. A favorite hobby can be turned into a lucrative second income if you go about it the right way. Ask someone in the know for some expert advice. Doing something that you have a passion for can be the key to your financial success.

43rd Week/October 22–28

Wednesday the 22nd. Your financial picture can take an unexpected turn for the better. This may take place through the idea of an older man. His business ideas may seem unorthodox, but they work. If you take a chance now, you may reap a profit in the future. Finish up your work early and head to the gym for a good workout.

Thursday the 23rd. The people around you are very sociable, so take time out to stop and chat. You can become privy to some valuable office gossip if you keep your ear to the ground. Romantically speaking, you may find yourself attracted to someone very intelligent at this time. Keep your eyes open at the bookstore or lecture hall.

Friday the 24th. Out with the old and in with the new; that should be your motto. This is the perfect time to clear out the old clutter in your house and office. It may also be time to let go of a relationship that isn't working. Drop a friend who no longer seems to have your best interests at heart.

Saturday the 25th. Whatever you begin today can show profit within about a month. This should be an especially good time to purchase real estate or to move into a new home. If money is a concern, put the word out to loved ones, and someone is likely to come through with a loan. Entertain friends at home this evening.

Sunday the 26th. Romance may be high on your list of priorities. This is a perfect time for an intimate brunch with a loved one, followed by a lazy stroll through the park. Those of you who are looking for a new place to live should have luck this afternoon. You may need to look at a few places before finding the perfect one, however.

Monday the 27th. You may be required to use your creative abilities on the job. If this is new territory for you, you may be surprised at your own latent talent. If this is what you usually do, expect to exceed even your own expectations. Guard against pressing your opinions on others. Leave room for everyone to have a viewpoint.

Tuesday the 28th. You will be in the mood for fun after a busy time at work. Finish work early and join a friend for an adventure. Go biking or hiking in the woods, or go on some rides at the amusement park. You may be the recipient of a prize of some sort right now. You may hold the winning lottery ticket, or the winning bingo card.

Weekly Summary

You excel at communications at the present. This should be a good week to sell yourself or to sell a product to others. Schedule job interviews or company reviews now to ensure a successful outcome. Discussions with loved ones may not go very well, as you may be more detached than you are compassionate. Wait until you get back to normal.

You can find joy in domestic pursuits this week. Embark on home renovation or repair projects. You can enjoy updating or redecorating a room or two. Add a fresh coat of paint, or consider changing the paint color completely for a brand-new look. Even just purchasing a small scatter rug can brighten things up.

A relationship may be on the verge of becoming serious. A loved one may want to make a permanent commitment to you. If you feel it is too soon, now is the time to speak up. You can feel a little rushed right now. There should be nothing wrong with taking things a little more slowly.

44th Week/October 29–November 4

Wednesday the 29th. You should feel ambitious and motivated to achieve. A work conflict may result in a showdown, but you will be in a better position once the dust settles. Taking a romantic risk now is likely to pay off, so don't be shy. You may find that you are most attracted to people by their integrity.

Thursday the 30th. You may be more perceptive than usual at this time, perhaps even bordering on psychic. As a result, making decisions can be easier; just avoid second-guessing yourself. Your first instinct probably is the best choice. A long-term career wish may be granted at this time, as friends in high places seem to be on your side.

Friday the 31st. Communication may be the key to ironing out a minor conflict in your primary relationship. Avoiding the issue will only make things worse. Consider getting away for a short trip with a friend or loved one. Perhaps a change of scenery is just what you need at this time. New experiences with new people can help you to broaden your perspective.

Saturday November 1st. You may be craving new and different experiences. Do something exciting that you and your partner can participate in and learn together. A stronger bond and a renewed sense of passion can emerge as a result. Enjoy the company of some off-the-wall people this evening at a party thrown by a fun friend.

Sunday the 2nd. This is one of those days when you want peace and quiet. Hang out with an intelligent yet reflective friend this afternoon. It should feel nice to be with someone who is so supportive and accepting of you as you are. A love relationship may seem idyllic right now, but avoid putting your beloved up on a pedestal lest he or she should topple off.

Monday the 3rd. You may need to be on your guard at work. One of your colleagues may be jealous of you and can very well try to take credit for your work. Confront the person on it. This is a good day to eliminate the clutter that may have gathered around you. Clean and clear out and organize closets and drawers.

Tuesday the 4th. You will be seen as compassionate and caring if you respond to a friend in need. Appreciation is a reward in itself. A love relationship is gaining momentum. Get out of your own way on this one. If you fear something, talk to your beloved and be reassured. Urge neighbors to vote this Election Day.

Weekly Summary

This is a good week for working on your daily routine of health and diet. It may be that your hectic schedule does not allow you a lot of time in this capacity. Streamlining may be the key to success right now. Consider consulting with a professional nutritionist to set up a routine that works the best for your lifestyle.

You may be deciding whether or not to take on a partner in a business. Doing everything on your own may be appealing right now, but it may not be financially practical. A partner could add to the level of expertise that you have to offer, and could also help to keep you down-to-earth. Someone with integrity and loyalty should help you to succeed.

Money matters may be your top priority this week. If you have any accrued debt, this is a good time to deal with it before it gets out of hand. Even if you cannot pay it off now, plan how you can achieve this goal in the future. A greater sense of personal power should be the result.

45th Week/November 5–11

Wednesday the 5th. You can be very persuasive now. This is a good time to ask people for favors, or to sell your ideas to others. You can see the bigger picture, and this broad perspective will allow you to make plans for your future. It may seem as if you have the gift of prophecy.

Thursday the 6th. Whatever you do, you can do very quickly. Avoid becoming impatient with slower types right now, however. Working independently will allow you to do things at your own pace. If you must travel in connection with your work or your education, consider squeezing in a few days of fun as well. You may have friends near your destination.

Friday the 7th. You may be seen as an expert in your field just now and be called upon to give some advice. Soak up the admiration of your fans, and accept this recognition of your skill and expertise. Friends will prove their reliability and loyalty to you this evening if you trust them with a secret.

Saturday the 8th. Expect things around you to be somewhat hairy. You will feel more emotional than usual right now, and the people around you appear to be very intense and unpredictable too. An issue with a loved one may come to a head, but this should enable you finally to get to the heart of the matter and resolve it.

Sunday the 9th. You are sure to want to keep busy and productive. Spend time on a pet project, or jump into chores around the house. A reliable friend will be good company this afternoon, so go along shopping for appliances, household goods, or for quality items that you plan to keep for a long time.

Monday the 10th. You are in demand now, so be sure to take your cell phone with you when out and around. This is a day to make plans and to coordinate your efforts with those of others. Your communicative abilities tend to be enhanced right now. You can do very well in dealings with all, bigwigs and children alike.

Tuesday the 11th. You do your best work in a group setting now. Bounce ideas off colleagues or friends to get feedback. You may be seen as unconventional, but your ideas are ahead of their time. Your natural magnetism is enhanced, so don't be surprised if you are approached by someone very attractive. You may attend a patriotic ceremony.

Weekly Summary

Perhaps you are planning the trip of a lifetime. This is a great time to go; freedom is your priority this week. You can broaden your perspective on life by visiting cultures that are exotic and different. If getting away is impossible right now, become an armchair traveler and plan a trip for when you can.

A job change may have been the last thing on your mind until you get a call out of the blue from a headhunter. Consider the possibilities if you were to take on this challenge. This opportunity can have you doing something completely out of your area of expertise. The significant raise in pay is something to consider as well.

You find satisfaction from participating in group activities. Volunteer your organizational and leadership skills to your favorite charity or community groups. Getting involved will make you feel needed and useful. You can make new friends and enjoy more social activity as a result of your participation.

46th Week/November 12–18

Wednesday the 12th. You seem to have the gift of discipline at present. Rewards will come your way when you employ patience as well. You can build things now. This can be a good time to physically construct something, to do renovations around the home, or to build your body through exercise. If a child makes a mistake, praise whatever has been done right.

Thursday the 13th. Household tasks are more likely than usual to bring satisfaction. Income can be made from domestic activities at this time. Consider starting up a home-based business, or play host to foreign exchange students for a few months. Interacting with people from a different culture can be just as rewarding for you as it is for them right now.

Friday the 14th. Watch your pocketbook. You may be more inclined than usual to overspend right now. If you do not take a list with you when out shopping, you will come home with a variety of new and exciting, although expensive, products. Entertain friends at home this evening, with either a formal dinner party, or a potluck supper.

Saturday the 15th. Things have a better chance than usual of going your way. Be direct and ask for what you want. Your skills of communication also are enhanced, so your luck may be doubled in the areas of negotiation and conversation. Don't be afraid to bargain with salespeople when purchasing large ticket items now.

Sunday the 16th. You will want your own space this weekend. Independent action is what excites you now, so venture forth under your own steam. You may also excel at sports and physical pursuits. This may be a good time to take up a new game, specifically one that allows for one-on-one, or head-to-head competition.

Monday the 17th. You will be more intense and focused than usual. Expect to get much accomplished as a result, but you must stick with one or two major projects. Your love life may be quite intense at the moment. A love interest may be pressuring you in some way. Speak up now and make it known exactly where you stand with things.

Tuesday the 18th. You have a strong work ethic at present and can expect a lot from yourself. Ease up a little bit, however. You will perform at your optimum level when you put less pressure on yourself. Tend now to routine health matters that you may have been putting off. Make appointments for checkups with the doctor and the dentist.

Weekly Summary

You may be inclined to seek out the company of friends this week. Perhaps you have been too reclusive lately, and now feel a need to expand outward. Consider having a get-together in your home, and invite a few people over. This should be a good way to get the ball rolling and to garner a few reciprocal invitations as well.

You may be thinking about taking on a roommate at this time. It can be a platonic roommate, or perhaps a love interest. Realize that you may need to agree on some rules beforehand in order to make this work. You need a lot of personal space now, so be sure that you get the alone time that you require.

A business opportunity may come to your attention through a family friend. Even though the individual may seem to be supportive of the project, it will behoove you to do your own background investigating. There may be a detail or two that would not be to your liking. Trust your gut instinct on this one.

47th Week/November 19–25

Wednesday the 19th. You now may be more susceptible to temptation than you usually are. A risk that you would not normally even think of taking may seem quite feasible at this time. Ask for input first. This should be a favorable time to make travel plans, but don't pack too much in at once. Remember to allow yourself some time to rest too.

Thursday the 20th. Your social life probably will be perking up. Those around you seem to be in a chatty mood, so allow extra time for socializing when out and around right now. A sudden revelation from a male friend or relative can leave you bewildered this evening. Give yourself some time to get used to the idea. You may then see its benefits.

Friday the 21st. You want your privacy, and you make an effort to shun the spotlight. Try to arrange to work from home if at all possible. This can be a good time to set up a home-based business of some sort. You are quite savvy when it comes to money, and you can probably see the financial benefits of working from your own home.

Saturday the 22nd. Those of you who are in the market for a new home should view some open houses this weekend. You can be lucky enough to find one that fits your budget and your taste. A sacrifice may have to be made in some minor area however, but all the major concerns should be covered. Attend a family celebration of some sort this evening.

Sunday the 23rd. This should be an incredibly auspicious time for new beginnings. A trip taken now can lead you down some unexpected highways, but should also be the adventure of a lifetime. If you are single, a new romance may enter your life and change it forever. Some of you may welcome the addition of a new child to your life.

Monday the 24th. You probably will find yourself the center of attention for some kind of creative work or project. You radiate confidence and warmth right now, and your audience should be a very appreciative one. Get involved in some kind of recreational activity this evening. Join the kids in whatever they are doing now.

Tuesday the 25th. It may be necessary to find a constructive outlet for your assertive tendencies. If you don't channel them well, they will transform into anger or irritation with other people. Physical labor or exercise can be one positive activity. Engaging in a competition of some type may also be a good way for you to feel powerful.

Weekly Summary

Your ability to adapt to others may be called into question this week. Going along with the crowd may not be easy for you right now. Compromise is the key. Realize that things don't have to be all their way, or all your way. Give a little and take a little. An easy camaraderie can be had if you are open to the possibilities.

You may be the recipient of a myriad of social invitations now. You are lucky enough to have the stamina and the motivation to attend most of them, so go for it. Burning the candle at both ends at this time can be easily remedied as long as you don't overdo it. Keep children entertained by introducing them to some arts and crafts.

You excel at things requiring attention to detail and fine craftsmanship at this time. If you work with your hands, your skills may be noticed by an important client. An extraordinary offer may come your way as a result. Consider it carefully, as the financial reward can be significant as well.

48th Week/November 26–December 2

Wednesday the 26th. You are seen as efficient and productive just now. A project that you thought was completed may not be ready to be put away quite yet. More work may need to be done at the last minute. A friend may approach you to volunteer your services for a charity drive. Take part, as new friends can be made as a result.

Thursday the 27th. Business may intrude on the early part of this Thanksgiving Day, but you should be able to resolve the problem quickly by compromise. Then you will be free to feast on good food and good conversation with those you love. Use tact and diplomacy when asking a friend for a favor this evening, and it is likely to be granted to you.

Friday the 28th. Your primary relationship can be a source of comfort and harmony. Allow your mate to take the lead in making plans for the evening. It is likely that his or her choices will work out in both of your best interests better than yours would at this time. A legal victory may not yield as much profit as you had hoped for.

Saturday the 29th. You especially enjoy the company of friends and groups this weekend. Take part in a trade show connected to your career, or organize or participate in a charity race or walkathon. You probably are considered unconventional right now, but you may really just be ahead of your time. Put your ideas out to different people to get different responses.

Sunday the 30th. You may be thinking twice about a decision made just one week ago. A glitch in your plans can be causing you some concern right now, but a minor adjustment in strategy may be all that is needed to get things back on track. Your intuitive ability is enhanced at this time. Your dreams tonight can contain a solution to a problem.

Monday December 1st. Your intuition can be a valuable guide at present. Trust it when deciding about whether or not to take action on an investment opportunity. If an appliance is acting up, check the warranty. Call the company immediately, and you might be able to get it at no expense to you.

Tuesday the 2nd. You will be noticed for your glamour and natural attractiveness. Dress for success and wow a group of bigwigs in a meeting this afternoon. A confident attitude can go a long way toward getting what you want right now. Avoid being seen as too bossy with a friend now, however. Give people some room to express themselves as well.

Weekly Summary

Your primary relationship is a priority for you this week. A mate may complain that you're being too possessive, and this can leave you bewildered. Making the issues clear between you will restore harmony and happiness once again. Things tend to work out in your favor now, so this can be a great time to sign contracts or to buy important items.

You may find that money has been flowing out faster than it has been flowing in lately. Your generous nature can have gotten the best of you this holiday season, and you may have overextended yourself financially. You can minimize the damage, and cut back on any interest accruing, by getting on top of things now. Make a plan and stick to it.

A sibling or good friend may ask you to make good on a promise that you had made previously. Don't let the person down; your good word can be at stake here. You may need to keep yourself busier than usual now. Your mind is quick, and you may need some extra mental stimulation.

49th Week/December 3–9

Wednesday the 3rd. Travel can be on your agenda right now. A friend may try to entice you to come along on an extended vacation. Although tempting, you must remember your responsibilities at home right now. Consider joining your friend on one leg of the journey instead. Physical exertion is likely to be good for your physical and mental health this evening.

Thursday the 4th. You may fall prey to the heady thrill of romance. If you are single, someone you meet at this time can become an important part of your life. If already partnered, you may feel a renewed surge of passion with your beloved. Plan something special for this evening. A dinner out with candlelight should do the trick.

Friday the 5th. You may be in a more serious frame of mind than usual. You are concerned about your emotional and financial security at this time. Take whatever measures are necessary to bring you peace of mind. If a business isn't showing profit, it may be time to let it go. Don't hang on simply out of pride.

Saturday the 6th. This is a good day to shop for furniture, clothing, or anything of quality that you want to last for a long time. You can run into some good bargains, so shop and compare to get the best deal. You do appreciate the little luxuries of life right now, so splurge on some special treat for yourself.

Sunday the 7th. You can be networking with a wide variety of people now. Keep plans flexible to accommodate your changing moods. Variety may be the spice of life these days; so you may be involved in a wide mix of activities. You may be asked to take part in a neighborhood block party or a block watch program this evening.

Monday the 8th. You are feeling more emotionally volatile than usual. You may notice that the people around you seem to be quite tense and reactive as well right now. A confrontation with an irritating co-worker may be unavoidable at this time. In fact, clearing the air now can be the best thing for both of you.

Tuesday the 9th. Expect to have a fateful encounter. You may meet someone new, but it will feel as if you have known the person your whole life. This man or woman can become a lifelong friend or a significant love interest. Avoid expecting too much from relatives at this time. Realize that they can do only what they can do right now.

Weekly Summary

You perhaps will want to break out of your rut this week. It may be best to control your impatience, however. Your eagerness to change may cause you to make some decisions that you will later regret. Allow yourself some time to become clear on what it is that you really want in your life before making some impulsive major decisions.

A job offer may come your way out of the blue this week. This can be a golden opportunity for you to expand your abilities and your talents. It can also be very lucrative. There also are ways for you to find new responsibilities within your existing position. Either way, change is inevitable for you at this time.

Take part in some local and community group efforts right now. You may want to expand your social circle, and this can be a great way for you to do it. Find something that has meaning for you, and volunteer some time to it. You can make a difference, and a wonderful feeling of accomplishment is its own reward as well.

50th Week/December 10–16

Wednesday the 10th. Lie low and take things easy. You can especially enjoy treating yourself well right now. Browse through the bookstore and pick up the latest bestseller, or schedule a message for yourself this afternoon. This is a good time to meditate or to practice any kind of spiritual or religious discipline. Spend some time with your family this evening.

Thursday the 11th. Avoid getting pulled into a power play at work. A colleague may try to recruit you into supporting his side. Remain neutral to come out on top. Your discipline and focus may be nothing short of remarkable at this time. You are very likely to achieve whatever it is that you set your sights on.

Friday the 12th. Lady Luck is on your side. Taking risks can produce a bigger pay-off than usual at this time, but don't go overboard. Expressing your opinion to a friend can leave you feeling distraught. If the individual reacts defensively, remember that it is more likely to be about him or her than it is about you. Rephrase to get a different response.

Saturday the 13th. Things should run along smoothly. You will feel in harmony with friends and family at this time. Spending some time alone may be imperative to your sense of well-being, however. You should enjoy taking up a new sport or activity. Learn to ski with the kids, or engage in something competitive.

Sunday the 14th. You can be quite discriminating in your tastes at this time. Some people might even call you picky. Having high standards is nothing to be ashamed of, but avoid expecting too much from others. You can appreciate more cultural events. Attend a wine tasting event this afternoon, as your palate seems to be finely tuned.

Monday the 15th. You probably will be involved in making a major financial transaction, and it can prove to be a good move on your part. You can profit from investments in items of beauty and culture. Consider precious gemstones or artwork. You can display and enjoy these kinds of investments around your home as long as there is adequate security.

Tuesday the 16th. You may be seen as someone who is on the ball. You have the ability to nab a promotion, a competitive offer, or a new client right now. With extra money coming in, this can be a good time to structure a budget. Stop at the organic food store and cook a healthy dinner this evening.

Weekly Summary

You may learn more by keeping a low profile for a while. If you have a nagging feeling that something in your working life or your personal life is wrong, trust that feeling. Retreat to the background until the players in your life reveal themselves to you. A secret may come to light. Once done, you can make some conscious and clear choices.

Your natural leadership ability can cause you to come across as rather bossy. Try to maintain an attitude of equal cooperation instead of leadership. Realize that you may be more intimidating than you think. Closing business deals should be a snap now if you turn on your considerable charm.

Money matters can be a big part of the picture right now. Your naturally generous nature may lead you to spend more on gifts than you originally intended. The recipients will love your generosity, but it is you who will have to deal with the credit card bill. Revamping the budget ahead of time can help you to integrate the extra expenditures now.

51st Week/December 17–23

Wednesday the 17th. You probably will be out and around a fair bit, running errands and the like. Expect to bump into somebody that you haven't seen for a long time. Renewing a friendship can brighten your day. You appreciate the beauty in your surroundings now. Visit an art gallery, or treat yourself to a facial or manicure.

Thursday the 18th. Communication confusion can turn this day upside down. Double-check all appointment times, and allow extra travel time as well. You may run into more traffic jams than usual. Don't be surprised if a lunch date stands you up; it seems to be becoming a habit. Avoid signing any important documents right now.

Friday the 19th. You may be given the opportunity to invest in a friend's idea. Although it may take a while before you see any profit, your friend will see your support as an act of faith. Your love life may switch into high gear this evening when a love interest showers you with attention. Soak it up.

Saturday the 20th. If you are celebrating Hanukkah, have a happy holiday. Others may be feeling a little stressed out thinking about what needs to be done for the holidays. You can relax once you get things organized. You can make lists, but realize that you cannot do everything at once anyway. Delegate responsibility to other family members as well. A party this evening should help you to get into the spirit of the season.

Sunday the 21st. You will wake up in an optimistic and cheerful mood this morning. Tackle chores and tasks early on, taking time out for fun this afternoon. This may be a good day to go skiing or sledding with the family. Friends may drop by unexpectedly later on, so be sure that the pantry is well stocked with snacks.

Monday the 22nd. Your unconventional solution to a an old problem at work can make you the center of attention. You may be seen as brilliant by some, and as radical by others. It may be more difficult than usual to be pinned to one project or location right now. Try to focus on work that allows you some freedom of movement.

Tuesday the 23rd. If you begin something now, be prepared to see good results within the month. This should be an auspicious time to begin thinking about future career goals, and how to achieve them. Consult people in the field. Their experience can give you invaluable information. Keep your ears perked for office gossip during a Christmas party this evening.

Weekly Summary

This week an investment opportunity may be presented to you through a friend. Think twice before jumping in. Don't let the opinions of others sway your sound judgment. In fact, your judgment on this matter is likely to be more realistic than theirs. It may be prudent to pass on this deal, and in the process save your friend his money as well.

You may be preparing for a verbal presentation at this time. Public speaking is something that you would rather avoid if at all possible. Once you get up there, however, you will glory in the attention and power that you are able to command. Practice a few times with a friend, and you should have no problems at all.

Your family ancestry may be fascinating to you right now. Consider putting together a family tree. You can pass this on down the line to your own offspring. Researching this can even put you in touch with relatives whom you never have met. It can open up a whole new world for you to explore. Expect to end up doing some traveling as a result of your piqued interest.

52nd Week/December 24–31

Wednesday the 24th. You have to be quite industrious, for you are going to be kept busy tending to various tasks and chores on your to-do list. Your charm and magnetism are magnified right now, so go out to a party thrown by a friend this evening. If you are single, your chances of meeting someone wonderful will be very high.

Thursday the 25th. Merry Christmas! If the family is around this morning, things should go fairly smoothly. One relative in particular may make a special effort to please you now. Reciprocate any kindness. You may find that you meet a lot of new people now, as friends of friends drop in for a quick visit. You should feel happy and contented this evening.

Friday the 26th. Even if you were planning on having a quiet day, it is not likely to work out that way. Expect to be kept busy and on the go with friends and family. Take visiting relatives sightseeing, or hit the after-holiday sales. You can find some amazing bargains right now, especially in the area of home electronics.

Saturday the 27th. Just as the financial impact of the season is hitting you, you may receive a financial windfall. A friend can repay a debt from long ago, perhaps one that has been long forgotten. A tax refund or insurance settlement may arrive in the mail, or a relative may decide to give you a large financial gift.

Sunday the 28th. You feel more assertive than usual. Channel this energy constructively to prevent it from coming out in inappropriate ways, such as anger or irritation with other people. Watch your driving. A lead foot is bound to lead to a speeding ticket, and you probably will not be able to talk your way out of it.

Monday the 29th. You probably will be up early, ready to tackle whatever comes your way. You find that you do best in short, but productive, spurts. Starting things with enthusiasm and energy is what you do best at this time, but finishing them as well can be a bit of a challenge. Get some physical exercise this evening.

Tuesday the 30th. You may be rethinking a decision that you made several days ago. Don't throw in the towel just yet. Improvise a little bit, and things may turn out even better than anticipated. A love interest may seem too good to be true right now. Avoid putting anyone up on a pedestal, however. Unrealistic expectations can lead only to disappointment.

Wednesday the 31st. Now, more than usual, you feel like you need to go along with the ideas of other people. This may not be a good day to fight for what you want. Do your best to compromise with others now, and a win-win situation can result. Spend the evening with trusted and close friends, perhaps at a small dinner party.

Weekly Summary

You can get a lot of pleasure being with your love this week. If you are single, you want even more to find that special someone soon, especially with the holiday season upon us. The single Leo must trust that the right person will show up when the time is right. You will meet someone sooner than you think.

Try to stick to a budget when going on any shopping expeditions this week. It may be too easy to be impulsive and buy whatever tickles your fancy right now. Your thinking is very ingenious now, so you can think of new and creative ways to make money. One of these ideas may actually work to your advantage. Ask a smart friend for advice.

The idea of travel may excite you right now. In fact, getting out of town for the holidays can be a good idea. Some of you may enjoy a warm, tropical beach in some exotic land. Getting away to the heat can do much to rejuvenate a Leo mind and body. You might be able to find some last-minute deals at a good price.

DAILY FORECASTS:
JULY–DECEMBER 2002

Monday July 1st. Handling money on behalf of other people can be successful if you are very careful to go by the book. Do not take any risks. A friend could confide secrets which you would rather not have heard. Devote some to a relative down on their luck.

Tuesday the 2nd. It might be quite difficult reaching friends for a chat, leaving you feeling rather lonely. A work meeting could be lengthy and somewhat tiring, but with a little extra effort you should be able to arrive at some useful decisions.

Wednesday the 3rd. This is a period for attending to other people and ignoring your own needs. Be sure to get some extra exercise, even if you walk around the block. Memories of happy times when you were younger should not be allowed to spoil the present.

Thursday the 4th. If you have to travel to a conference, leave early. You could make useful contacts during coffee hour before the official business begins. A new and better job in the communications industry might be the way to get ahead if you feel stifled at work.

Friday the 5th. Your personal ambitions may be rather hazy, even unrealistic. It is fine to aim high, but set your sights on a reachable goal. There may be some difficulties with parents or in-laws due to opposite opinions that are far apart. Try to be tolerant.

Saturday the 6th. Today is a starred time for whisking youngsters off for a special day. Keep your destination secret, and watch their faces light up as the surprise is revealed. All social events are favored. If you want to make new friends, there are chances to do so.

Sunday the 7th. Relax happily in company with a few old friends. Although you might be inspired to focus on tasks around the house, they are likely to be left unfinished. Catch up on letter writing.

Monday the 8th. The dividing line between friendship and love is hard to define. Whatever your feelings, stay within the bounds of decent behavior. Going around in old clothes is not going to impress colleagues, so take a bit more pride in your appearance. Tests may be more challenging than you expected.

Tuesday the 9th. Close relationships are under the microscope, and feelings of boredom or even indifference must be faced. Try to recapture that old thrill. This is not the best time to begin a strict health regime.

Wednesday the 10th. A fresh approach to your self-development brings renewed enthusiasm. Today is excellent for beginning to study meditation or yoga. Generosity to other people by giving either time or money will be rewarded. Check on a pet, or you might have to pursue a wanderer.

Thursday the 11th. Do your best to keep your head down and get on with your own work, particularly if you are struggling to meet a deadline. If someone you used to know turns up and seems eager to be friends, you might not be as happy about it as they expect.

Friday the 12th. There is no point trying to conceal a misdemeanor from your mate or partner. A legal entanglement should be avoided if at all possible, since a court case may not come out in your favor. A poetic, romantic image may appeal but could look odd.

Saturday the 13th. Today is excellent for taking care of personal chores and for shopping; you should be able to whiz through in record time. A delightfully romantic evening is foreseen if you are prepared to splurge on good theater or concert tickets.

Sunday the 14th. It would be preferable to stay home this morning and do a bit of tidying up, leaving you free to call friends and chat for as long as you want. Sporting events may be a letdown, but that is no reason not to play to win. Be wary of forcing the issue in a romantic relationship; play a little hard to get.

Monday the 15th. Financial work should go very smoothly, although you might have to insist on not being interrupted. An old habit may melt away without you realizing what is happening, since your life has changed so much. Work out or go for a vigorous jog. You will benefit from being more physically active.

Tuesday the 16th. If you have to sell an idea or a product, your Leo enthusiasm is bound to carry the day. It would be kind to give a lift to a neighbor or a relative who is without transportation. Expand your social circle by taking up a new leisure interest that will bring you into contact with a wider range of people.

Wednesday the 17th. If you act on your principles no matter how difficult the dilemma, you cannot go far wrong. Old friends could bring a sense of security into your life. Expect to find it more challenging than usual to work in private. You will need to make an extra effort to keep your mind from wandering.

Thursday the 18th. Love might have already led you to a partner without you even realizing it. Feelings of affection cannot be denied for much longer. Today is ideal for planning big changes to the look of your home. Do not believe every promise a colleague makes, nor inducements from a higher-up.

Friday the 19th. The end of the workweek allows you to relax a little more as a big project draws to an end. This is a good cause for celebration after work. If you are putting your house on the market you could get a buyer almost immediately.

Saturday the 20th. You enjoy rushing around feeling needed and wanted. A new diet should be working. An inner conviction that there is more to life than material possessions should not be ignored. Focus on what you need, not on what other people have.

Sunday the 21st. If you intend to visit a sick relative or friend, try to do so this morning. Events later in the day might conspire to stop you. By evening you could be feeling restless and in need of a change. Throw out or give away clothes that long ago went out of style. Pare down the number of your possessions.

Monday the 22nd. Today's period of relative calm allows you to introduce a new colleague to your regular working practices. You might become friends along the way. Consider buying a new cookbook, then experimenting with unusual recipes.

Tuesday the 23rd. Your individual talents ought to receive extra attention, as you are praised by someone who is not normally so effusive. Today is good for forging a new link with your mate or partner by allowing them to see your vulnerabilities. Spoil yourself a little by buying some new clothes or accessories. Stay close to the phone this evening.

Wednesday the 24th. It is necessary to be patient if you are hoping for a special invitation. Use a subtle approach rather than being demanding or manipulative. Financial risks should be avoided. Today is not a very promising time to take a test because you could be overconfident and not well prepared.

Thursday the 25th. You may be inclined to blurt out angry words, but this will only hurt other people. It is better to say nothing rather than upset anyone unnecessarily. Youngsters are likely to be demanding. A dreamlike atmosphere could pervade a social event, making you wonder what is actually real.

Friday the 26th. That special person in your life may seem unable to come out with what they apparently want to say. Try to ease their way. If you rush off in a hurry this morning you might forget to take your keys or wallet or you might miss appointments.

Saturday the 27th. It would be tempting to betray a friend's confidence when you are told a juicy secret. Their trust in you must be respected. Be careful when playing sports to stick to the rules of the game. Romance will come your way in its own time. Love cannot be manufactured.

Sunday the 28th. Morning is the best time for discussing tricky topics with your loved ones. Just make sure you do so with sensitivity. If you lose an item at home, it will probably turn up eventually. Minor symptoms of illness should not be ignored; look after yourself tonight and you will probably feel fine in the morning.

Monday the 29th. This is an ideal day to make your mark at a new job assignment as long as you do not step on anyone's toes in doing so. A romantic encounter could lead to further dates, but only if you have the courage to make your interest clear. All leisure pursuits are highlighted, offering much creative pleasure.

Tuesday the 30th. Your personal dynamism will be useful in solving a training problem that needs a special touch. Although a risky bet is not often recommended, today you could gamble a small sum and walk away with a handsome profit.

Wednesday the 31st. With friends, when you are trying a new cultural interest and do not enjoy it, there will be no need for pretense. Leos who work for a charity might find it profitable to look for funding overseas. Allow your instincts to guide you if asked to speak in a large meeting. You will be much less effective reading from a prepared script.

Thursday August 1st. If colleagues and loved ones seem short-tempered, it could be that you are getting on their nerves by being overbearing. Generosity is vital today, so do not stint with money or other gifts. Be careful not to eat too much if you go out this evening. Stick to dishes you have tried before.

Friday the 2nd. Do not allow a lawyer to pull the wool over your eyes with jargon. You have a right to understand every aspect of a legal matter in which you are involved. Someone who at first appears very attractive could turn out to be quite ordinary. Cut back on expensive social events for a while.

Saturday the 3rd. This is a starred time to be with youngsters. Taking yourself seriously is the first step toward being respected by other people. An invitation to dine with a couple you admire could make you a little nervous, but they will soon put you at ease.

Sunday the 4th. Angry words could be out of your mouth before you realize what you are saying. Be careful. There may be a problem with an electrical item at home, which you should get an expert to fix. Youngsters must not be allowed to get away with rudeness or bad manners. Teach them by example.

Monday the 5th. You may be unwilling to get into your chores this morning. However, the sooner you start, the quicker you will be finished. A meeting could be tense but eventually productive. A greater sense of responsibility is developing in you. Begin to think more about caring more for friends and family members.

Tuesday the 6th. There is an irresistible air drawing attention to you today, so if you are hoping for a date go ahead and ask. It is unlikely that you will be disappointed. Spare-time hobbies are favored. Relax with a favorite pastime. You might be surprised and delighted to win a prize in a competition.

Wednesday the 7th. This is an ideal day to get to know new neighbors. If you have long wanted to get an article published try doing so now and you just might be lucky. Love sometimes needs to be expressed clearly before a relationship can become deeper and more meaningful to both partners.

Thursday the 8th. Renew yourself by altering your image. A new hairstyle should prove rejuvenating. Today is excellent for enhancing your reputation at work by learning skills that no one else in the office currently possesses. Hopes of a romantic encounter may be fulfilled when you bump into someone special.

Friday the 9th. An old friend could prove invaluable. Being the center of attention does not usually make you nervous, so it should not be a problem to speak to a work meeting on a serious topic. Go out separately from your mate or partner tonight, giving each other a little personal breathing space.

Saturday the 10th. You are apt to get out of bed in a rather grumpy mood this morning. Shopping should not be done hastily, especially if you are trying on clothes. Be patient with children and loved ones, no matter how much they test the limits of your temper.

Sunday the 11th. A quiet start to the day might frustrate your plans to go out, since everyone seems too lazy to rush. You, too, will soon slow down to a more relaxed pace. An opportunity to benefit a friend or relative by sharing your knowledge on a particular topic should not be a signal for you to show off.

Monday the 12th. All writing is favored this morning, and the work will probably be pleasurable. You are apt to be in quite an extravagant mood, so leave your credit cards at home if you are trying to save. Telling your mate or partner the depths of your feelings can brighten your whole relationship.

Tuesday the 13th. You are beginning to achieve some special personal goals and should feel very positive. Today is a good time for getting around town since traffic conditions and parking should be relatively easy. Youngsters might be bored and need entertaining.

Wednesday the 14th. There is no point asking too high a price for your house or car if you need to sell, especially if you are hoping for a quick offer. Be careful that you are not manipulating loved ones to do what you want without realizing it. The chance to make some extra cash in your spare time should not be turned down, even if you highly value your free hours.

Thursday the 15th. You may find out the hard way that love cannot be bought, after throwing every luxury at someone who just is not interested in a long-term relationship. If you enjoy creative writing, be prepared to hit a few times when your imagination is taking a rest. It is better to keep quiet than to look a fool by offering opinions you have not thought out.

Friday the 16th. Create the right romantic surroundings to ask for a commitment. Today could mark the beginning of a new and closer relationship. Ideas for a business to be run by you and a colleague may seem off the wall at first. With a few modifications, you might come up with a lucrative plan.

Saturday the 17th. There is no excuse for trying to force children to obey you. Kindness should be the rule at all times. All sporting events are favored. If you are playing on a team, pull out all the stops. Money could vanish unless you get your priorities straight.

Sunday the 18th. Romance can be happy as long as you keep your expectations within reason. Let what happens, happen. A little light housework would be worthwhile. Or cook an unusual meal using some ingredients you have never tried before.

Monday the 19th. Friends will rally round in times of need. A meeting you have been dreading is likely to turn out surprisingly well. You may come out with your reputation enhanced. Relations with neighbors might be strained by thoughtless behavior.

Tuesday the 20th. It is fine to assert yourself, but if you overdo it people will be needlessly irritated. Hopes of winning a legal case might be slightly unrealistic. Try to keep an open mind concerning the eventual outcome. Set aside time to be by yourself when no one can make demands on you.

Wednesday the 21st. This is an ideal time to introduce a new romantic partner to friends and family. A sense of idealism will guide you through a battle of wills at work. Allow yourself to think differently from colleagues. Opinions are not carved in stone, and it is wise to stay open and adaptable in your thinking.

Thursday the 22nd. A turning point in your closest relationship has been reached, and it is up to you to now find the way to proceed. This must be a shared enterprise, of course. Money can be made thanks to an unusual opportunity a friend tells you about. Creatively there has rarely been a more dynamic time.

Friday the 23rd. Getting your finances in order may seem boring but is essential. Do some organizing to find out how much you are worth. Today marks the beginning of a period when you should put extra effort into keeping physically fit and healthy. Intriguing research absorbs your attention.

Saturday the 24th. Youngsters may seem a little solitary and lonely. Encourage them to go out and play. When a social event is canceled it can be a relief. This is not an ideal time for impulsively jumping into a committed relationship. If you truly love each other, there is no need to hurry the process.

Sunday the 25th. A personal dream can come true as long as you go out of your way to make it happen. Sporting events should be quite exciting. You will probably be happier playing rather than watching. Turn in a performance of which you can be proud.

Monday the 26th. You may have to plunge in at the deep end this morning, but with such a worthwhile project that you are energized. All communication is favored. This is an ideal day for making difficult phone calls or writing a letter of condolence.

Tuesday the 27th. Although you may be a little more sensitive than usual to criticism this morning, it is bound to be meant in a positive, helpful way. All travel is favored, particularly if you are with a colleague or a loved one. Be prepared for pleasant surprises.

Wednesday the 28th. This morning bodes well for a job interview. If you present an image of a steady, reliable worker, you have a good chance of being selected. Putting money into a personal project is worthwhile as long as you have the support of your loved ones.

Thursday the 29th. Today is especially promising for Leos who are looking for a new job. Scour the want ads, and send off as many applications as you can manage. It would be wise to check that all your insurance policies are properly covered.

Friday the 30th. If you and your boss do not see eye-to-eye, you may have to back down. You certainly should not stir up trouble that could be avoided. A close friend may be angry and best left to work out their feelings on their own.

Saturday the 31st. Today is an excellent time for hosting a party, especially if you want to get back in contact with old friends. Shopping for yourself is favored, although you might be tempted to buy a rather expensive item. Your outgoing mood makes you good company.

Sunday September 1st. If neighbors invite you to drop by for a friendly chat, it would be rude to refuse. You may be introduced by a friend to someone very attractive. A sense of responsibility toward loved ones might lead to your giving up a personal pleasure.

Monday the 2nd. Financial paperwork should be easy to handle, even if you have been dreading doing so. Find time to help out a colleague who has gotten out of their depth with a complicated task. Your Leo powers of persuasion are quite strong today.

Tuesday the 3rd. Good news reaches you regarding a close relative, with the possibility of an invitation to a special event very soon. You may be romantically attracted to someone outside your usual social circle. Unusual ideas for business might appeal to your adventurous side but need to be carefully investigated.

Wednesday the 4th. Your Leo intuition is quite powerful at the moment. People could be astonished at your understanding of their emotions. Early signs of a youngster's artistic talent should be encouraged, but gently so that the element of fun is not lost. If friends bring up unusual topics of conversation, do not reveal more than you want the world to know.

Thursday the 5th. Talking about love with friends may be almost enough to arouse the feeling itself. Spending money on social events may be enjoyable, but try to build up some savings also. Eat fairly plain food today, and avoid alcohol as well as too much caffeine. Be sure to take prescribed pills.

Friday the 6th. Becoming a parent, or even thinking about doing so, can be an experience that makes you grow up very quickly. You then have to learn that someone else's needs always come first. Today is a promising time for public speaking. Stay close to home this evening, and get to bed reasonably early.

Saturday the 7th. Today's rather foreboding atmosphere may make you feel pleasure is out of the question, but that is not the case. Just do not take leisure activities and sports lightly. A new start with a romantic affair is favored, even if each of you is uncertain how the relationship will turn out.

Sunday the 8th. The main focus is on the family. Minor quarrels among loved ones can be healed just by spending time together. Take a look around your home to see if some furnishings need to be replaced. While shopping, opt for the best you can afford.

Monday the 9th. An aptitude test should give you no problems. If you have been thinking of buying a new car, start choosing a model and then comparing options and prices. A romantic encounter could leave you blushing and embarrassed, but this show of emotion may just charm the other person.

Tuesday the 10th. Because you are more organized than usual, it will be easy to get daily chores out of the way and to phone friends at a distance. Look around antique shops and thrift stores to pick up some interesting pieces. Loved ones can cheer you with a display of affection.

Wednesday the 11th. It is not always possible to get everything right in a close relationship, but there is no need to compound the error. If you have made a blunder, admit it and apologize. Today is not promising for a family celebration. Your visionary mood should allow you to rise above common problems.

Thursday the 12th. Creative ventures ought to go particularly well. The more time you can spare for your favorite artistic pursuit, the better. Where romance is concerned, guard against analyzing too much. Just let the warmth of emotion sweep you along. Children can be great fun. Join in their games if you are invited.

Friday the 13th. This morning is a good time to take an exam. A small bet could make you a winner, but do not get into the habit of gambling. Social events to which you have been invited may appear shallow, and you would prefer serious conversation.

Saturday the 14th. Calls may be few, allowing you to get on with weekend chores. A letter could go astray, so do not be surprised if you have not received an answer to one you sent a few weeks ago. Allow youngsters to play their own games quietly without trying to impose adult standards on them.

Sunday the 15th. Health matters are apt to be on your mind, putting you in the mood to get some extra exercise. Today is a pleasant time for puttering around the house, completing minor tasks that loved ones have wanted done for ages. Cooking a special meal can be a way of showing your love and affection.

Monday the 16th. Leos who are starting a new job might feel a little nervous, but there is no reason to be upset. New colleagues will prove helpful. An elderly relative might appreciate being given a cat or dog as a loving companion, but check first. Look into alternative or complementary health care.

Tuesday the 17th. If your mate or partner seems sensitive this morning, do not just say toughen up. Respect your loved one's feelings as you expect your own to be respected. Business dealings that appear even slightly shady should be avoided. You are unlikely to benefit in any way from dishonesty. Find time to let your imagination roam and to dream of what is to come.

Wednesday the 18th. As a matter draws to an unexpectedly sudden conclusion, you may be left to face the consequences. These might not be exactly what you expected. Romantic matters must be handled very cautiously or you run the risk of a temporary separation.

Thursday the 19th. Although your love affair should be going well, this is probably not the most stable relationship you have ever had. Sooner rather than later your mate or steady date is bound to appear in a less romantic light. There is some risk of losing money, especially if you do not take care of your purse or wallet.

Friday the 20th. It is unlikely that you will be able to unwind as the weekend approaches. Last-minute work needs to be done urgently. The demands made upon you might be heavy. Do not be tempted to change your savings goals. Stick to your current budget.

Saturday the 21st. Parents may direct some criticism at you which seems unfair, but keep in mind that their criteria for judgment are different from your own. A social event might feel more like a burden than a pleasure unless you make a deliberate decision to have fun. Friends may introduce you to a romantic prospect.

Sunday the 22nd. When playing sports or exercising, do not get too carried away or you could strain a muscle and be laid up for a few days. A romantic date is probably not going to be the answer to all your dreams. In fact, you might find it quite hard to even get along with the person. Weekend tasks may have to be left unfinished if unexpected company drops by.

Monday the 23rd. A bright light is shining on your relationship with a brother or sister. Past disagreements should be forgotten. It would be wise to check your car for potential trouble. New neighbors add zest to the locality and may become your friends.

Tuesday the 24th. There is no excuse for spending a lot of money on yourself when items for your home are needed. Do not be greedy. Today's very sociable atmosphere makes it ideal for entertaining guests at home. A kind word will go a long way toward patching up a strained relationship.

Wednesday the 25th. Being overly ambitious is not going to serve your purposes in the long run, so keep your career aims within realistic limits. You may be respected by colleagues, but that means little unless loved ones hold you in esteem as well. The urge to stay home this evening could be overruled by the need to be seen at a public function.

Thursday the 26th. A sudden change of direction at work could catch you unaware, making it somewhat difficult to adjust to new responsibilities. Do not try to patch up old or faulty electrical equipment; just replace the item with a brand-new one.

Friday the 27th. All written work is highly favored. If you have a report to turn in, you may well receive praise for it. Check through any contract before signing, although there should be few if any problems. Youngsters may need a little extra encouragement with schooling, especially if they are in a new school.

Saturday the 28th. The prospect of a blind date might not be as alluring as when you first agreed to it. It would be wise not to expect too much. This is not the most successful time for creative attempts. If you are trying to sell what you make, be prepared for an uphill struggle. A new friend could brighten your day.

Sunday the 29th. On this quieter day you will enjoy talking over old times with friends. Group activities such as a trip or a picnic might prove quite tiring and rather disappointing. However, it will do you good to have a change of scene. Youngsters may seem determined to try your patience, so be quite firm.

Monday the 30th. Sooner or later you will get down to work. Try to find time to do some clearing out at home, especially of old clothes and outdated accessories. It would be thoughtful to get in touch with a relative or a distant friend who may be lonely.

Tuesday October 1st. Inspiration is the name of the game. Utilize your excellent Leo imagination on a new project. If you are attracted to someone, do not expect them to intuit your feelings; tell them so. A change of image may suit you to a youthful, casual look. Experiment with colors and styles.

Wednesday the 2nd. It may be necessary to go over the details of a financial deal again because an error might have crept in. Maintain your efforts to stay physically fit. Youngsters will benefit from knowing the exact bounds on their behavior. Do not let them rule you or even start to get the upper hand.

Thursday the 3rd. Sometimes it is not possible to make the impression you want on someone special. Your best chance of success is probably not to try too hard. Just be your natural self. Money might be causing you a few anxious moments, and this is not an ideal time to either loan or borrow funds.

Friday the 4th. Today is an excellent time for considering ways to renovate your home. Go out and make your selections. Romance may be nearer than you think; someone you see often is on the brink of asking for a date. Overindulgence should be avoided. You will only regret it if you put on additional weight.

Saturday the 5th. Today's main focus is on your sense of security, whether this is based on accumulating material goods or on emotional bonding. Act so that you feel protected against the foreseeable accidents of life. Social events might not be as attractive as shopping. An advertised sale may offer irresistible discounts.

Sunday the 6th. There is little chance of being bored. Invitations are apt to come for organized activities. You can make a new start with neighbors who have been annoying you recently by being more tolerant. Practice the fine art of forgiving.

Monday the 7th. An exciting new work project could spark your interest. Your ideas will be welcome. All contractual agreements are favored, although you should look carefully through the paperwork. You may be able to make new friends by studying the personals but do not expect to find love that way.

Tuesday the 8th. Make the most of today by building confidence in your own creative abilities. Whatever you do best, vow to take it to a higher level. Romance is favored, although a date may turn out to be more emotional than you ever expected. Try not to lose the sense of fun you enjoyed as a carefree child.

Wednesday the 9th. You may have to revisit a work problem that you thought had been solved, and this time it must be sorted out once and for all. Family disagreements can be put to rest if you have the patience to talk them out. Youngsters could need a bit of encouragement at school.

Thursday the 10th. If you are in the middle of buying a house, do not expect that all will go smoothly. There may still be problems to overcome. Recent purchases that no longer look good should be returned to the store for a refund or exchange. Love gone underground at the moment will emerge again.

Friday the 11th. Work meetings are likely to be demanding, and may even require you to stay late. If friends offer perhaps harsh criticisms, they have other matters on their mind. There is no point being too rigid in expressing your morals and ideals; ease up when circumstances suggest a lighter approach.

Saturday the 12th. Looking after your health you acquire an attractive glow, which you will realize when you begin to receive compliments. This quiet, domestic day does not rule out the possibility of meeting new people in the neighborhood.

Sunday the 13th. Short trips are apt to cause some upset, particularly if youngsters are irritable. If entertaining friends, keep the preparations simple so you are able to relax with them. Get your financial paperwork in order and you may find some spare cash.

Monday the 14th. Not all of your colleagues are going to agree with you if you come up with quite radical plans, so be prepared to struggle to win their support. There is no point trying to force yourself to enjoy art forms that do not appeal, such as modern music. Have the confidence to stand out and be different.

Tuesday the 15th. Getting around your neighborhood might be more of a problem than usual due to road repairs and heavy traffic. Just remember to keep cool and not lose your temper. This is an excellent time for resolving to run or jog daily, or even to walk.

Wednesday the 16th. New computer technology could force you to spend quite a lot of time learning it. In the long run, however, it should make your job easier. Aspiring Leo photographers should take some experimental shots before the light fades. Enjoy a social night out with friends who know you well.

Thursday the 17th. If you offer support to a family member, be there in a time of need. Do not let them down by forgetting your promise. There is little point throwing good money after bad if you have made a mistake in decorating a room. Unrealistic hopes of a romantic partner can be shattered, but if you expect less they will not disappoint.

Friday the 18th. Clearer lines of communication between you and your mate should ensure that a recent argument fades into insignificance. Love does not always have to be expressed in words. Sometimes a look is enough, or a thoughtfully chosen gift. Luck is at your side this evening in a game of chance.

Saturday the 19th. If you planned to go out for the day, expect a few disruptions to your schedule. It would be wise to check your car before setting off. A brother or sister could upset you concerning a matter of principle, but do not let this sour your relationship.

Sunday the 20th. A close relationship is about to take a distinct turn for the better. You may have renewed interest in practicing a rhythmical exercise such as yoga or aerobics. As a Leo beauty is important to you, so do not starve it out of your daily life.

Monday the 21st. It is make-or-break time with a course of study, so determine that you will do well. Travel for business should be productive. The temptation to start a new life in a far-off place is an alluring dream. Do not make a snap decision.

Tuesday the 22nd. If you are collaborating with friends on a joint creative project, today is ideal for making some plans. A meeting at work to discuss an advertising campaign may be a bit unusual for you, but there are ways to make a definite contribution.

Wednesday the 23rd. Bring current jobs to a successful conclusion. You ought to be able to get along better with your parents, particularly if they reveal stories from their past which arouse your sympathy. Check locks and alarm systems around the house.

Thursday the 24th. Normally it is not wise to rush a written report, but right now you are able to work at maximum speed without compromising quality. A more active approach to finding friends will soon enlarge your social circle, so get out and mingle.

Friday the 25th. Your natural Leo optimism can help a local pressure group organize a campaign effectively. If you receive compliments for your style, accept them gracefully but do not become arrogant. Be wary of even speaking to a child who is alone.

Saturday the 26th. Ideas for socializing could come from friends who have lived in countries where the customs vary from your own. Today is excellent for a family get-together. Make your home a welcoming place for friends and neighbors even if they just drop by.

Sunday the 27th. Your personal self-development is about to take a big leap forward, particularly due to your creative ambitions. Find time to plan how to become a more fulfilled person. Romance should be smooth sailing at the moment. The emotional bond between you and your mate or partner is getting stronger.

Monday the 28th. Travel conditions are promising. You should have little difficulty getting around the neighborhood. If you are engaged in legal matters as part of your job, today may mark a breakthrough. New ideas for bringing together far-flung members of the family could galvanize relatives into positive action.

Tuesday the 29th. This quite busy day may keep you on your toes, allowing little time to go into any subject very deeply. Toward day's end, however, you may realize that someone you met earlier has made a deep and romantic impression on you. You will not get away with keeping the truth from loved ones.

Wednesday the 30th. Be careful when choosing furniture for your home. What attracts you in the showroom might look quite different in your house. Family relations will improve if everyone gives a little more and expects to take a little less. A dating partner may forget to show up as arranged.

Thursday the 31st. You should be feeling so positive this morning that no task is too much or is even daunting. A quick search through a few antique shops could reveal a good-looking ornamental piece or a vase which you cannot resist. Romance is on the brink of becoming real. Savor the delicate moments.

Friday November 1st. Be a little restrained with your spending or you might drain one of your bank accounts. There is nothing to be gained by setting yourself up against a colleague who has greater experience than you; it is better to be modest and low-key.

Saturday the 2nd. Try to remember your dreams when you wake up. They might hold a valuable clue that will help you solve a minor current problem. Your mate or partner would appreciate a surprise gift or a night out on the town. Shopping could cause you to lose your temper, so keep the trip short.

Sunday the 3rd. With a bright day lying ahead, try to get up earlier than usual and make the most of it. You are eager to bring family members together, which should prove successful. Creative pursuits will almost certainly be satisfying, as you uncover progressively deeper springs of imagination.

Monday the 4th. At last the breakthrough you have been waiting for is about to come as a business associate offers an invitation that is hard to refuse. Legal affairs that have not been going well may now unexpectedly take a turn for the better.

Tuesday the 5th. You cannot afford to be anything but honest today, so own up to any mistakes you made recently. Keep a watchful eye on youngsters for any sign that they are getting into some sort of trouble. Say nothing rather than putting your foot in your mouth when asked for an opinion. Study all the options before rendering a verdict.

Wednesday the 6th. You can float through any and all difficulties without even realizing they are present. It should not be hard to find inspiration for creative projects, either for your own pleasure or for work. If you are taking a test, allow your good Leo intuition free rein as well as relying on your reasoning powers.

Thursday the 7th. If you are looking for a secondhand car, check out what is being advertised. Try not to be negative or sarcastic about colleagues. Doing so is not kind. Reading or listening to music can reveal more of the meaning of life as you tune into yourself. Heed your inner voice.

Friday the 8th. A friend may be stonewalling you for reasons that are hard to figure out. It would probably be best to leave them alone, and wait for time to work a change of heart. You may be given a chance to work for an idealistic organization, but it may mean a cut in salary. Think long and hard about this.

Saturday the 9th. Family matters should take precedence over your own concerns, although you are unlikely to willingly give up your freedom today. This is not the easiest of times to entertain at home. Do not try too hard to impress anyone. Having faith in the future can create a more optimistic outlook.

Sunday the 10th. Your high level of energy gives you verve and enthusiasm which can be very attractive. Go play some sports, even if you do not usually enjoy competing. All types of practical work around the house are favored. Take the initiative to get a romantic affair off the ground; shyness will not help.

Monday the 11th. Making a clear decision might be a problem. Your first instinct will be to plunge right into challenging situations, but then a more cautious mood will urge you to draw back. A neighbor may suggest setting up a babysitting co-op or other services, which would be useful as well as fun.

Tuesday the 12th. There are apt to be some welcome personal messages among the many business notes. Find time to read the latest novel or nonfiction book that is topping the best-seller list. Your faith in a friend may be shaken.

Wednesday the 13th. This less rushed day will be like an oasis in the middle of a busy week. There are financial questions that can be cleared up if you concentrate. If you have a secret you are bursting to tell whispering it to a pet should get it off your mind without betraying any confidences.

Thursday the 14th. Leo parents should make youngsters the focus of attention. There is a lot you can do to supplement what they learn at school, but be subtle about it. If you are moving, all should go according to schedule. Do not interfere.

Friday the 15th. A clash between your personal desires and your assigned duties at work could cause you a few anxious moments. Of course, you know which must come first. A social event may not be very exciting, putting you close to total boredom. However, it is important to be polite and not depart too soon. Older friends can offer good advice.

Saturday the 16th. Slow down this morning. Just do what you have to do, and take your time. Youngsters may have to be told quite firmly that money does not grow on trees. You might fall in love with someone because they have a mesmerizing voice.

Sunday the 17th. Your mate may seem lost in a private world, so that it is difficult for you to make contact. You may have been too much in each other's company; a period of withdrawal will not hurt your relationship. Enjoy fully your favorite music.

Monday the 18th. A job interview may be so different from what you expect that you are quite put off. However, if you can keep your senses you will probably do well. Your reputation might be on the line concerning a local affair. It is vital to stand up for what you believe in despite heavy opposition. Try not to be taken in by a new colleague's pretense of knowing it all.

Tuesday the 19th. A new interest in arts and crafts could pleasantly fill some of your free hours even if you do not reach a high level of excellence. Children are apt to be full of fun, so join in their games even if people stare. Love can be returned in full measure if you make it clear you feel strongly. There is no need to repress your romantic emotions.

Wednesday the 20th. Loved ones might complain that you are spending too much time at work, and they probably have a point. Overtime may be eating into evening hours. Colleagues will work better if you organize together into a well-oiled team.

Thursday the 21st. After a long period when you felt you would never win love, it seems that special person is coming around. Take the next few days carefully, and not rush toward a commitment. If you are trying to sell your house, do not lower your asking price. A good offer may be made much sooner than you think.

Friday the 22nd. Today marks the start of a few weeks when you will be feeling much more competitive than usual. That is fine if you want to get ahead at work, but do not become ruthless. All matters of the heart are highlighted; you might receive a pleasant surprise in the mail. You could also be lucky in a competition.

Saturday the 23rd. Break out of the mold of weekend routine and go somewhere new and different. It will do you a lot of good to feel the wind in your hair and let your worries dissolve. New friends could invite you to dinner, giving you a chance of getting to know each other better. Keep in touch with relatives.

Sunday the 24th. It would be ideal to exercise both your body and mind, perhaps by playing some sport and enjoying some good conversation at the same time. Youngsters will probably amaze you with their imaginative powers. Enjoy a drink with friends tonight.

Monday the 25th. Ending a relationship is never easy. However, when it becomes clear what has to be done, do not put it off. Be kind and get it over with quickly but gently. Shopping for yourself might be tiring, because it is hard to find clothes that really appeal. Do not waste money.

Tuesday the 26th. Get into the swing early so you can beat competitors to the punch. This is a good time for socializing, but you might be surprised at the seriousness of the subjects that come up. Developing more faith in yourself is an essential part of maturing, which is happening naturally.

Wednesday the 27th. News of an old friend might not be all good, but at least it will be great to be back in touch. Allow plenty of time to get to appointments, and do not panic if you run a little late. All meetings at work are favored, particularly if you have ideas to offer regarding advertising and communications.

Thursday the 28th. This quite demanding day will probably tire you out, but it should give you much satisfaction as well. Keep work in its place; do not allow it to begin to dominate your personal life. Youngsters can ask some very awkward questions.

Friday the 29th. If you are a little short of funds at the moment, it might be wise to turn down an invitation to an extravagant social event. Nor is this a good time to borrow money, since paying it back might prove difficult. Catch up with friends by phoning or visiting.

Saturday the 30th. Romance is at a point where the right word can save the relationship. If you have been hesitating about making a commitment, be aware that further delay may end your chances. Pursuing leisure interests and sports that require expensive equipment can be a drain on your budget, so carefully weigh the cost. An evening out may bring secrets to light.

Sunday December 1st. Sudden inspiration to change the look of your home can be a good thing, but do not be too hasty. Relations within the family might be a bit touchy now. The simplest remedy is to stay out of each other's way. Today is ideal for getting together with friends and letting your hair down.

Monday the 2nd. If you have to take the blame for someone else's mistake, you are bound to feel resentful. Make it clear that they owe you a favor in return, which you will definitely collect. Affairs of the heart should be treated with caution. The person you want may be quite different from what you imagine.

Tuesday the 3rd. If you must move at this time of the year, expect a few disruptions to your plans and some breakage, too. It will not help to be hasty when trying to conclude a work project. Just take as much time as you need, and do not panic. Try to stay out of legal matters, or at least try to arrange a quick settlement. Do not let a disagreement escalate into a fight.

Wednesday the 4th. Happily, a new love affair is in the cards for Leo singles. You may meet someone who is totally different from anyone you have ever known. Creative work should go extremely well. Getting on the bathroom scale could give you a bit of a shock.

Thursday the 5th. Be sure to encourage youngsters who show an early interest in music or art. Do not take the fun out of it, however, or you will only turn them off. Today is promising for all competitive situations. You will never be happy in love if you cannot make up your mind between two different people.

Friday the 6th. Today should be reasonably quiet, allowing you to catch up. Although you and that special someone might not be in the first throes of passion, the deeper affection that arises over time should prove a great pleasure and comfort.

Saturday the 7th. Set aside some time to be with the one you love most. Wild partying probably will not appeal so much as sitting down with friends to a good meal, preferably one you cooked yourself. The more relaxed you are, the happier your guests will be.

Sunday the 8th. Dreams may stay in your mind longer than usual this morning, making it difficult to concentrate. Write down as much as you remember, but do not try to figure out the meaning just yet. Although this can be a very romantic day, you need to set up the right situation in order to enjoy love fully.

Monday the 9th. Trying to manipulate loved ones is not going to work, primarily because they know you so well. It would be unwise to risk any money as you are almost certain to lose a bet. A sudden burst of creativity could be a revelation, giving you more confidence in your native talent than ever before.

Tuesday the 10th. You may become aware of an opportunity to retrain and expand your skills. Do not even think about whether to do this; just go for it. If you go all-out to impress someone attractive, they are very unlikely to refuse any offer you make. No matter what may be worrying you, remaining cheerful will be very strengthening.

Wednesday the 11th. You might be remembered in a will. However, there are likely to be a few legal hitches before you actually receive the legacy, so do not spend in advance. There is no point entering into a rivalry; find a way of cooperating. Keep in the background where romance is concerned, and stay out of trouble.

Thursday the 12th. Friends are not always in a position to help you with a personal plan. Try to realize that. Research might take more time than expected, but do not allow that to put you off. Sometimes it is wiser to keep emotions to yourself rather than express them and precipitate a lengthy disagreement.

Friday the 13th. Today offers a mixture of mixed-up communications and clear intuition. Make sure that you have been understood when issuing instructions. Youngsters could try the patience of a saint. This is an ideal evening for going to a concert or dancing.

Saturday the 14th. When choosing gifts, think of what people would like rather than what appeals to you. A romantic encounter may make your heart beat faster, giving you a lot to dream about. An actual date, however, might disappoint both of you.

Sunday the 15th. You may feel a little weary when you first wake up, so it would be wise to pace yourself. Close relationships come under the microscope. You and your mate or partner might benefit from an intimate conversation. Invite a few friends for an informal meal, gossip, and companionship.

Monday the 16th. Many Leos expect to be busy. The secret to success is to hurry slowly; do not allow yourself to be rushed. Meetings ought to be quite productive, and new ideas may be proposed. An old friend could present an entirely new side of personality that strikes an immediate chord in you.

Tuesday the 17th. Contradictory forces are at work in your closest relationship, causing you to long for freedom and togetherness at the same time. This dilemma may not be resolved, but it can be contained. Do not be too hard on friends if they do not share all of your opinions. Listen; you could learn something.

Wednesday the 18th. You are beginning to find a philosophy of life that really suits you. Becoming a true individual is the most exciting quest you will ever go on. A romantic occasion could lead to a relationship that marks a turning point in the way you understand love. Express your private emotions in prose or verse, but keep what you write to yourself.

Thursday the 19th. A friendship has reached the point where you either become much closer or have to part. The choice is not entirely yours. If you spend more time with loved ones and less on the go, everyone will be happier. This is not the best day to join a club or society because you could get involved in one which is being torn apart by internal rivalries.

Friday the 20th. If this is your last day at work for a while, try to get in early this morning. That will give you a head start so that there is no need to rush or to stay late. Turn your high energy to healthy use by jogging or going to a gym. Control your temper, especially if you get frazzled by crowds.

Saturday the 21st. You will probably be happiest being left alone, which might surprise loved ones. There is a lot of work you have to do in private. A former lover could get in contact, and you realize it is now possible to be friends. Stay at home this evening and treat yourself to welcome peace and quiet.

Sunday the 22nd. This is an ideal time for any domestic jobs, especially if you are preparing in advance for the next few days. Pets should occupy some of your attention; after all, you got them to bring you pleasure. Try not to give in to every whim a mate expresses.

Monday the 23rd. Getting through the morning might take gritted teeth, as loved ones seem to know exactly how to get on your nerves. The atmosphere will improve. There should be chance for you to shine in a group, thanks to a glittering social event. Generosity to those in need is particularly recommended now.

Tuesday the 24th. Expect an active day, but do not allow that to get in the way of contacting old friends. Make time to chat when you receive calls; do not be curt. Last-minute shopping trips could turn up some delightful and unexpected bargains.

Wednesday the 25th. Merry Christmas! You have organized so well that the day runs like clockwork. Some overindulgence is to be expected, of course. Just keep an eye on youngsters so that they do not make themselves ill. Bask in the love that fills the air.

Thursday the 26th. There is no need to struggle alone or to martyr yourself. Ask for help to lighten your burden. A short walk will clear your head. Friends who may not have many reasons to celebrate should be offered tactful sympathy and support.

Friday the 27th. Get an early start. Your car may not be in perfect working order. A partner would be delighted if you two sneak away as if you are having a secret liaison. A brother or sister may offer good advice on improving your style and image.

Saturday the 28th. The urge to take risks with your own safety is unwise, so keep clear of any dangerous sport. Find fun elsewhere, and do not frighten loved ones by taking foolish chances. Keep your temper if parents or in-laws get on your nerves.

Sunday the 29th. Just puttering around taking care of small jobs can be satisfying. Try not to let romance go out of your life. Keep your imagination in working order by frequent contact with art and music. Loved ones should be left to do their own thing.

Monday the 30th. Passion is virtually unavoidable today. If you have been yearning for romance, this could be the fulfillment of your dreams. Going to a friend's house for a meal could turn out to be quite exciting as you are introduced to artistic people.

Tuesday the 31st. What is most on your mind may be the future of your closest relationship. Happily, you and your partner are entering a phase of greater togetherness and understanding. Resolve to pursue your creative talents and to enjoy life more.

WHAT DOES YOUR FUTURE HOLD...?

DISCOVER IT IN *ASTROANALYSIS*—

COMPLETELY REVISED TO THE YEAR 2015, THESE GUIDES INCLUDE
COLOR-CODED CHARTS FOR TOTAL ASTROLOGICAL EVALUATION,
PLANET TABLES AND CUSP CHARTS, AND STREAMLINED INFORMA-
TION FOR ANYONE WHO HAS EVER LOOKED TO THE STARS AND
WONDERED....

__ARIES	0-425-17558-8/$12.95
__TAURUS	0-425-17559-6/$12.95
__GEMINI	0-425-17560-X/$12.95
__CANCER	0-425-17561-8/$12.95
__LEO	0-425-17562-6/$12.95
__VIRGO	0-425-17563-4/$12.95
__LIBRA	0-425-17564-2/$12.95
__SCORPIO	0-425-17565-0/$12.95
__SAGITTARIUS	0-425-17566-9/$12.95
__CAPRICORN	0-425-17567-7/$12.95
__AQUARIUS	0-425-17568-5/$12.95
__PISCES	0-425-17569-3/$12.95